SKETCH OF THE SIKHS

SKETCH
OF
THE SIKHS;

A Singular Nation,

WHO INHABIT THE

PROVINCES OF THE PENJAB,

SITUATED BETWEEN

THE RIVERS JUMNA AND INDUS

BY

LIEUTENANT-COLONEL MALCOLM,
AUTHOR OF THE POLITICAL SKETCH OF INDIA

GYAN

Published by

GYAN

Gyan Publishing House
5, Ansari Road
Daryaganj, New Delhi-110002
Phone: 011-47034999, 9811692060
E-mail: books@gyanbooks.com

Distribution Network
gyanbooks.com
India, USA, Canada, UK, Australia, France

ISBN : 978-81-212-4025-3 (PB)
First Published, 1812

2nd Impression 2020

Printed at: Gyan Press, Delhi.

Sketch of The Sikhs
Author: Lieutenant-Colonel Malcolm

SKETCH

OF

THE SIKHS;

A Singular Nation,

WHO INHABIT THE

PROVINCES OF THE PENJAB,

SITUATED BETWEEN

The Rivers Jumna and Indus.

BY

LIEUTENANT-COLONEL MALCOLM,

AUTHOR OF THE POLITICAL SKETCH OF INDIA.

LONDON:

PRINTED FOR JOHN MURRAY, ALBEMARLE STREET,

By James Moyes, Greville Street, Hatton Garden.

1812.

ADVERTISEMENT.

This Sketch has already appeared in the eleventh volume of the Asiatic Researches: but, as that valuable work is not in common circulation, it is now republished; and may prove acceptable, as a short and clear account of an oriental people, of singular religion and manners, with whose history the European reader can be but little acquainted.

SKETCH OF THE SIKHS.

INTRODUCTION.

WHEN with the British army in the Penjáb, in 1805, I endeavoured to collect materials that would throw light upon the history, manners, and religion of the Sikhs. Though this subject had been treated by several English writers, none of them had possessed opportunities of obtaining more than very general information regarding this extraordinary race; and their narratives therefore, though meriting regard, have served more to excite than to gratify curiosity.

In addition to the information I collected while the army continued within the territories of the Sikhs, and the personal observations I was able to make, during that period, upon the customs and manners of that nation, I succeeded with difficulty in obtaining a copy of the Adi-Grant'h *, and of some historical tracts, the most essential parts of which, when I returned to Calcutta, were explained to me by a Sikh priest of the Nirmala order, whom I found equally intelligent and communicative, and who spoke of the religion and ceremonies of his sect with less restraint than any of his brethren whom I had met with in the Penjáb. This slender stock

* The sacred volume of the Sikhs. The chief, who gave me this copy, sent it at night, and with either a real or affected reluctance, after having obtained a promise that I would treat it with great respect. I understand, however, that the indefatigable research of Mr. Colebrooke has procured not only the Adi-Grant'h, but also the Dasima Padshah ka Grant'h; and that, consequently, he is in possession of the two most sacred books of the Sikhs.

of materials was subsequently much enriched by my friend Dr. Leyden, who has favoured me with a translation of several tracts written by Sikh authors in the Penjábí and Dúggar dialects, treating of their history and religion; which, though full of that warm imagery which marks all oriental works, and particularly those whose authors enter on the boundless field of Hindú mythology, contain the most valuable verifications of the different religious institutions of the Sikh nation.

It was my first intention to have endeavoured to add to these materials, and to have written, when I had leisure, a history of the Sikhs; but the active nature of my public duties has made it impossible to carry this plan into early execution, and I have had the choice of deferring it to a distant and uncertain period; or of giving, from what I actually possessed, a short and hasty sketch of their history, customs, and religion. The latter alternative I have adopted: for, although the information I may convey in such a sketch may be very defective, it will be useful at a moment when every information regarding the Sikhs is of importance; and it may, perhaps, stimulate and aid some person, who has more leisure and better opportunities, to accomplish that task which I once contemplated.

In composing this rapid sketch of the Sikhs, I have still had to encounter various difficulties. There is no part of oriental biography in which it is more difficult to separate truth from falsehood, than that which relates to the history of religious impostors. The account of their lives is generally recorded, either by devoted disciples and warm adherents, or by violent enemies and bigotted persecutors. The former, from enthusiastic admiration, decorate them with every quality and accomplishment that can adorn men: the latter misrepresent their characters, and detract from all their merits and pretensions. This general remark I have found to apply with peculiar force to the varying accounts given, by Sikh and Muhammedan authors, of Nánac and his successors. As it would have been an endless and unprofitable task to have entered into a disquisition concerning all the points in which these authors differ, many considerations have induced me to give a preference, on almost all occasions, to the original Sikh writers. In every research into the general history of mankind, it is of the most essential importance to hear what a nation has to say of itself; and the knowledge obtained from such sources has a value, independent of its historical utility. It aids the promotion of social intercourse, and leads to the establishment of friendship between nations. The most savage states are those who have most prejudices, and who are consequently most easily conciliated or offended: they are always pleased and flattered, when they find, that those whom they cannot but admit to possess superior intelligence, are acquainted with their history, and respect their belief and usages: and, on the contrary, they hardly ever pardon an outrage against their religion or customs, though committed by men who have every right to plead the most profound ignorance, as an excuse for the words or actions that have provoked resentment.

SECTION I.

SKETCH OF THE HISTORY AND PRESENT STATE OF THE SIKHS; WITH OBSERVATIONS ON THEIR RELIGIOUS INSTITUTIONS, USAGES, MANNERS, AND CHARACTER.

NANAC SHAH, the founder of the sect, since distinguished by the name of Sikhs*, was born in the year of Christ 1469, at a small village called Talwandi†, in the district of Bhatti, in the province of Lahore. His father, whose name was Cálú‡, was of

* Sikh or Siesha, is a Sanscrit word, which means a disciple, or devoted follower. In the Penjábí it is corrupted into Sikh: it is a general term, and applicable to any person that follows a particular teacher.

† This village, or rather town, for such it has become, is now called Ráyapúr. It is situated on the banks of the Béyah, or Hyphasis.

‡ He is called, by some authors, Kálú Védí; but Védí is a name derived from his tribe or family.

the Cshatriya cast, and Védí tribe of Hindús, and had no family except Nánac, and his sister Nánaci, who married a Hindú of the name of Jayarám, that was employed as a grain-factor by Daulet Khán Lódí, a relation of the reigning emperor of Delhi. Nánac was, agreeably to the usage of the tribe in which he was born, married to a woman of respectable family, at an early age*, by whom he had two sons, named Sríchand and Lacshmí Dás. The former, who abandoned the vanities of the world, had a son called Dherm Chand, who founded the sect of Udásí; and his descendants are yet known by the name of Nánac Putráh, or the children of Nánac. Lacshmí Dás addicted himself to the pleasures of this world, and left neither heirs nor reputation.

* Several Sikh authors have been very precise in establishing the date of the consummation of this marriage, which they fix in the month of Asárh, of the Hindú æra of Vicramaditya, 1545.

Nánac is stated, by all Sikh writers, to have been, from his childhood, inclined to devotion; and the indifference which this feeling created towards all worldly concerns, appears to have been a source of continual uneasiness to his father; who endeavoured, by every effort, to divert his mind from the religious turn which it had taken. With a view to effect this object, he one day gave Nánac a sum of money, to purchase salt at one village, in order to sell it at another; in the hope of enticing him to business, by allowing him to taste the sweets of commercial profit. Nánac was pleased with the scheme, took the money, and proceeded, accompanied by a servant of the name of Bala, of the tribe of Sand'hu, towards the village where he was to make his purchase. He happened, however, on the road, to fall in with some Fakírs, (holy mendicants,) with whom he wished to commence a conversation; but they were so weak, from want of victuals, which they had not tasted for three days, that they could only reply to the observations of Nánac by bending their heads, and other civil signs of acquiescence. Nánac, affected by their situation, said to his companion, with emotion: "My father has "sent me to deal in salt, with a view to "profit; but the gain of this world is "unstable, and profitless; my wish is to "relieve these poor men, and to obtain "that gain which is permanent and eter-"nal." His companion* replied: "Thy "resolution is good: do not delay its exe-"cution." Nánac immediately distributed his money among the hungry Fakírs; who, after they had gained strength from the refreshment which it obtained them, entered into a long discourse with him on the unity of God, with which he was much delighted. He returned next day to his father, who

* Bala Sand'hu, who gave this advice, continued, through Nánac's life, to be his favourite attendant and disciple.

demanded what profit he had made? "I "have fed the poor," said Nánac, "and "have obtained that gain for you which "will endure for ever." As the father happened to have little value for the species of wealth which the son had acquired, he was enraged at having his money so fruitlessly wasted, abused poor Nánac, and even struck him; nor could the mild representations of Nánací save her brother from the violence of parental resentment. Fortune, however, according to the Sikh narrators of this anecdote of their teacher's early life, had raised him a powerful protector, who not only rescued him from punishment, but established his fame and respectability upon grounds that at once put him above all fear of future bad usage from his low-minded and sordid father. When Nánac was quite a youth, and employed to tend cattle in the fields, he happened to repose himself one day under the shade of a tree; and, as the sun declined towards the west, its rays fell on his face, when a large black snake*, advancing to the spot where he lay, raised itself from the ground, and interposed its spread hood between Nánac and the sun's rays. Ráy Bolar†, the ruler of the district, was passing the road, near the place where Nánac slept, and marked, in silence, though not without reflection, this unequivocal sign of his future greatness. This chief overheard Cálú punishing his son for his kindness to the Fakírs. He immediately entered, and demanded the cause of the uproar; and, when informed of the circumstances, he severely chid Cálú for his conduct, and

* The veneration which the Hindús have for the snake is well known; and this tradition, like many others, proves the attachment of the Sikh writers to that mythology, the errors of which they pretend to have wholly abandoned.

† Ráy, a title inferior to that of a Rájah, generally applied to the Hindú chief of a village, or small district.

interdicted him from ever again lifting his hand to Nánac, before whom, to the astonishment of all present, he humbled himself with every mark of the most profound veneration. Though Cálú, from this event, was obliged to treat his son with more respect than formerly, he remained as solicitous as ever to detach him from his religious habits, and to fix him in some worldly occupation; and he prevailed upon Jayrám, his son-in-law, to admit him into partnership in his business. Nánac, obliged to acquiesce in these schemes, attended at the granary of Daulet Khán Lódí, which was in charge of Jayrám; but though his hands were employed in this work, and his kindness of manner made all the inhabitants of Sultánpúr, where the granary was established, his friends, yet his heart never strayed for one moment from its object. It was incessantly fixed on the Divinity; and one morning, as he sat in a contemplative posture, a holy Muhammedan Fakír approached, and exclaimed: "Oh Nánac! upon what are thy "thoughts now employed? Quit such oc-"cupations, that thou mayest obtain the "inheritance of eternal wealth." Nánac is said to have started up at this exclamation, and after looking for a moment in the face of the Fakír, he fell into a trance; from which he had no sooner recovered, than he immediately distributed every thing in the granary among the poor*: and, after this act, proceeded with loud shouts out of the gates of the city, and running into a pool of water, remained there three days; during which some writers assert he had an interview with the prophet Elias, termed by the Muhammedans, Khizzer, from whom he learnt all earthly sciences.

While Nánac remained in the pool,

* This remarkable anecdote in Nánac's life is told very differently by different Sikh authors. I have followed the narrative of Bhacta Mallí. They all agree in Nánac's having, at this period, quitted the occupations of the world, and become Fakír.

abstracted from all worldly considerations, holding converse with a prophet, poor Jayrám was put in prison by Daulet Khán Lódí, on the charge of having dissipated his property. Nánac, however, returned, and told Daulet Khán that Jayrám was faultless; that he was the object of punishment; and that, as such, he held himself ready to render the strictest account of all he had lost. The Khán accepted his proposal: Jayrám's accounts were settled; and, to the surprise of all, a balance was found in his favour; on which he was not only released, but reinstated in the employment and favour of his master. We are told, by the Sikh authors, that these wonderful actions increased the fame of Nánac in a very great degree; and that he began, from this period, to practise all the austerities of a holy man; and, by his frequent abstraction in the contemplation of the divine Being, and his abstinence and virtue, he soon acquired great celebrity through all the countries into which he travelled.

There are many extravagant accounts regarding the travels of Nánac. One author*, who treats of the great reform which he made in the worship of the true God, which he found degraded by the idolatry of the Hindús, and the ignorance of the Muhammedans, relates his journey to all the different Hindú places of pilgrimage, and to Mecca, the holy temple of the Muhammedans.

It would be tedious, and foreign to the purpose of this sketch, to accompany Nánac in his travels, of which the above-mentioned author, as well as others, has given the most circumstantial accounts. He was accompanied (agreeable to them) by a celebrated musician, of the name of Merdana, and a person named Bála Sand'hú; and it

* Bhai Guru Vali, author of the Gnyána Ratnávali, a work written in the Sikh dialect of the Penjábí.

is on the tradition of the latter of these disciples, that most of the miracles* and wonders of his journies are related. In Bengal, the travellers had to encounter all kinds of sorcerers and magicians. Poor Merdaná, who had some of the propensities of Sancho, and preferred warm houses and good meals to deserts and starvation, was constantly in trouble, and more than once had his form changed into that of a sheep, and of several other animals. Nánac, however, always restored his humble friend to the human shape, and as constantly read him lectures on his imprudence. It is stated, in one of those accounts, that a Rájá of Sivanáb'hu endeavoured to tempt Nánac, by offering him all the luxuries of the world, to depart from his austere habits, but in vain. His presents of rich meats,

* Though his biographers have ascribed miracles to Nánac, we never find that he pretended to work any: on the contrary, he derided those who did, as deriving power from evil spirits.

splendid clothes, and fair ladies, only afforded the Sikh teacher so many opportunities of decrying the vanities of this world, and preaching to the Rájá the blessings of eternal life; and he at last succeeded in making him a convert, and resided at Sivanáb'hu two years and five months; during which period he composed the Prán Sancali*, for the instruction of his followers. After Nánac had visited all the cities of India, and explained to all ranks the great doctrines of the unity and omnipresence of God, he went to Mecca and Medina, where his actions, his miracles, and his long disputations with the most celebrated Muhammedan saints and doctors, are most circumstantially recorded by his biographers. He is stated, on this occasion, to have maintained his own principles, without offending those of others; always professing himself the enemy of dis-

* It is believed that this work of Nánac has been incorporated in the first part of the Adi-Grant'h.

cord, and as having no object but to reconcile the two faiths of the Muhammedans and Hindús in one religion; which he endeavoured to do by recalling them to that great and original tenet, in which they both believed, the unity of God, and by reclaiming them from the numerous errors into which they had fallen. During his travels, Nánac was introduced to the emperor Báber*, before whom he is said to have defended his doctrine with great firmness and eloquence. Báber was pleased with him, and ordered an ample maintenance to be bestowed upon him; which the Sikh priest refused; observing, that he trusted in him who provided for all men, and from whom alone a man of virtue and religion would consent to receive favour or reward. When Nánac returned from his travels, he cast

* This interview must have taken place in 1526 or 1527; as it is stated to have been immediately after Daulet Khán Lódí had visited Paniput, in 1526; where that prince had fought, and subdued Ibrahim, emperor of Hindústan.

off the garments of a Fakír, and wore plain clothes, but continued to give instructions to his numerous disciples; and he appears, at this period, to have experienced the most violent opposition from the Hindú zealots, who reproached him with having laid aside the habits of a Fakír, and with the impiety of the doctrines which he taught. These accusations he treated with great contempt; and an author, before cited, Bhai Gúrú Das Vali, states, that when he visited Vatála, he enraged the Yógíswaras* so much, that they tried all their powers of enchantment to terrify him. "Some," says this writer, "assumed the "shape of lions and tigers, others hissed "like snakes, one fell in a shower of fire, "and another tore the stars from the firma-"ment;" but Nánac remained tranquil: and when required to exhibit some proof of his powers that would astonish them, he

* Recluse penitents, who, by means of mental and corporeal mortifications, have acquired a command over the powers of nature.

replied: "I have nothing to exhibit worthy "of you to behold. A holy teacher has "no defence but the purity of his doctrine: "the world may change, but the Creator "is unchangeable." These words, adds the author, caused the miracles and enchantments of the Yógíswaras to cease, and they all fell at the feet of the humble Nánac, who was protected by the all perfect God.

Nánac, according to the same authority, went from Vatála to Multán, where he communed with the Pírs, or holy fathers of the Muhammedan religion of that country. "I am come," said he, when he entered that province, "into a country full of Pírs, "like the sacred Gangá, visiting the ocean." From Multán he went to Kírtipúr*, where he threw off his earthly shape, and was buried near the bank of the river Rávi, which has since overflowed his tomb. Kírtipúr continues a place of religious resort

* Kírtipur Dehra, on the banks of the Rávi, or Hydraotes.

and worship; and a small piece of Nánac's garment is exhibited to pilgrims, as a sacred relic, at his Dharmasálá, or temple.

It would be difficult to give the character of Nánac* on the authority of any account we yet possess. His writings, especially the first chapters of the Adi-Grant'h, will, if ever translated, be perhaps a criterion by which he may be fairly judged; but the great eminence which he obtained, and the success with which he combated the opposition which he met, afford ample reason to conclude that he was a man of more than common genius: and this favourable impression of his character will be confirmed

* He is, throughout this sketch, called Nánac. Muhammedan historians generally term him Nánac Shah, to denote his being a Fakír, the name of Shah being frequently given to men of celebrity in that sect. The Sikhs, in speaking of him, call him Baba Nánac, or Gúrú Nánac, father Nánac, or Nánac the teacher; and their writers term him Nánac Nirinkar, which means Nánac the omnipresent.

by a consideration of the object of his life, and the means he took to accomplish it. Born in a province on the extreme verge of India, at the very point where the religion of Muhammed and the idolatrous worship of the Hindús appeared to touch, and at a moment when both these tribes cherished the most violent rancour and animosity towards each other, his great aim was to blend those jarring elements in peaceful union, and he only endeavoured to effect this purpose through the means of mild persuasion. His wish was to recall both Muhammedans and Hindús to an exclusive attention to that sublimest of all principles, which inculcates devotion to God, and peace towards man. He had to combat the furious bigotry of the one, and the deep-rooted superstition of the other; but he attempted to overcome all obstacles by the force of reason and humanity. And we cannot have a more convincing proof of the general character of that doctrine which he taught, and the inoffensive light in which it was viewed, than the knowledge that its success did not rouse the bigotry of the intolerant and tyrannical Muhammedan government under which he lived.

Nánac did not deem either of his sons, before mentioned, worthy of the succession to his spiritual functions, which he bequeathed to a Cshatriya of the Tréhún tribe, called Lehana, who had long been attached to him, and whom he had initiated in the sacred mysteries of his sect, clothed in the holy mantle of a Fakír, and honoured with the name of Angad*, which, according to some commentators, means *own body*.

Guru Angad, for that is the name by

* This fanciful etymology represents the word Angad as a compound of the Sanscrit *Ang*, which signifies *body*, and the Persian *Khúd*, which signifies *own*. This mixture of language is quite common in the jargon of the Penjáb.

which he is known by all Sikhs, was born at the village of Khandúr, on the bank of the Béyah, or Hyphasis, in the province of Lahore. His life does not appear to have been distinguished by any remarkable actions. He taught the same doctrine as Nánac, and wrote some chapters that now form part of the Grant'h. He left two sons, Vásu and Dátu, but neither of them was initiated; and he was succeeded, at his death*, which happened in the year A. D. 1552, and of the Samvat 1609, by Amera Dás, a Cshatriya of the tribe of B'halé, who performed the duties of a menial towards him for upwards of twelve years. It is stated, that the daily occupation of Amera Dás was to bring water from the Béyah river, a distance of six miles, to wash the feet of his master; and that one night, during a severe storm, as he

* Angad died at Khandúr, a village about forty miles east of Lahore.

was returning from his journey, his foot slipped, and he fell and broke the vessel that contained the river water, opposite the door of a weaver, who lived next house to Angad. The weaver, startled at the noise, demanded, in a loud voice, of his wife, from whence it proceeded. The woman, who was well acquainted with the daily toils and the devotion of Angad's servant, replied, "It was poor Amera Dás, "who knows neither the sweets of sleep by "night, nor of rest by day." This conversation was overheard by Angad; and when Amera Dás came, next morning, to perform his usual duties, he treated him with extraordinary kindness, and said: "You "have endured great labour; but, hence-"forward, enjoy rest." Amera Dás was distinguished for his activity in preaching the tenets of Nánac, and was very successful in obtaining converts and followers; by the aid of whom he established some temporal power, built Kujaráwál, and separated from the regular Sikhs the Udásí sect, which was founded by Dherm-Chand, the son of Nánac, and was probably considered, at that period, as heretical.

Amera Dás had two children, a son named Móhan, and a daughter named Móhani, known by the name of B'háini; regarding whose marriage he is stated to have been very anxious: and as this event gave rise to a dynasty of leaders, who are almost adored among the Sikhs, it is recorded with much minuteness by the writers of that nation.

Amera Dás had communicated his wishes, regarding the marriage of B'háini, to a Brahmen, who was his head servant, and directed him to make some inquiries. The Brahmen did so, and reported to his master that he had been successful, and had found a youth every way suited to be the husband of his daughter. As they were speaking upon this subject in the street, Amera Dás asked what was the boy's stature? "About "the same height as that lad," said the Brahmen, pointing to a youth standing near them. The attention of Amera Dás was instantly withdrawn from the Brahmen, and intently fixed upon the youth to whom he had pointed. He asked him regarding his tribe, his name, and his family. The lad said his name was Rám Dás, and that he was a Cshatriya, of a respectable family, of the Sóndi tribe, and an inhabitant of the village of Góndawál. Amera Dás, pleased with the information he had received, took no more notice of the Brahmen and his choice of a son-in-law, but gave his daughter to the youth whom fortune had so casually introduced to his acquaintance*. Amera

* Though a contrary belief is inculcated by Nánac, the Sikhs, like the Hindús, are inclined to be predestinarians, and this gives their minds a great tendency to view accidents as decrees of Providence; and it is probable that this instance of early good fortune in

Dás died in the year A. D. 1574, and of the Samvat 1631, at the village of Góndawál, in the province of Lahore, and was succeeded by his son-in-law, Rám Dás*, whom he had initiated in the sacred mysteries of his holy profession, and who became famous for his piety, and still more from the improvements he made at Amritsar, which was for some time called Rámpúr, or Rámdáspúr, after him. Some Sikh authorities ascribe the foundation of this city to him, which is not correct, as it was a very ancient town, known formerly under the

Rám Dás, by impressing his countrymen with an idea of his being particularly favoured of Heaven, gave rise to an impression that promoted, in no slight degree, that success which it anticipated.

* No dates of the events which occurred during the rule of Rám Dás are given in any of the authorities from which this sketch is drawn. One author, however, states, that he lived in the time of Akber, and was honoured with the favour of that truly tolerant and great emperor.

name of Chak. He, however, added much to its population, and built a famous tank, or reservoir of water, which he called Amritsar, a name signifying the water of immortality, and which has become so sacred, that it has given its name, and imparted its sanctity, to the town of Rámdáspúr, which has become the sacred city of the Sikh nation, and is now only known by the name of Amritsar.

After a life passed in the undisturbed propagation of his tenets, in explanation of which he wrote several works, he died, in the year A. D. 1581, and of the Samvat 1638, at Amritsar, leaving two sons, Arjunmal and Bharatmal. He was succeeded by the former*, who has rendered himself

* Arjunmal, or Arjun, as he is more commonly called, according to B'hai Gúrú Dás B'halé, the author of the Gnyán Ratnávalí, was not initiated in the sacred mysteries of his father. This author says, that Arjun, though a secular man, did not suffer the office of Gúrú, or priest, to leave the Sóndi tribe. "Like a

famous by compiling the Adi-Grant'h *. The Adi-Grant'h, or first sacred volume of the Sikhs, contains ninety-two sections: it was partly composed by Nánac and his immediate successors, but received its present form and arrangement from Arjunmal †,

" substance," he adds, " which none else could di-" gest, the property of the family remained in the " family."

* Grant'h means book; but, as a mark of its superiority to all others, is given to this work, as " The " Book." Adi Grant'h means, the first Grant'h, or book, and is generally given to this work to distinguish it from the Dasama Padshah ka Grant'h, or the book of the tenth king, composed by Gúrú Góvind.

† Though the original Adi-Grant'h was compiled by Arjunmal, from the writings of Nánac, Angad, Amera Dás, and Rám Dás, and enlarged and improved by his own additions and commentaries, some small portions have been subsequently added by thirteen different persons, whose numbers, however, are reduced, by the Sikh authors, to twelve and a half: the last contributor to this sacred volume being a woman, is only admitted to rank in the list as a fraction, by these ungallant writers.

who has blended his own additions with what he deemed most valuable in the compositions of his predecessors. It is Arjun, then, who ought, from this act, to be deemed the first who gave consistent form and order to the religion of the Sikhs: an act which, though it has produced the effect he wished, of uniting that nation more closely, and of increasing their numbers, proved fatal to himself. The jealousy of the Muhammedan government was excited, and he was made its sacrifice. The mode of his death, which happened in the year of Christ 1606, and of the Samvat 1663, is related very differently by different authorities: but several of the most respectable agree in stating, that his martyrdom, for such they term it, was caused by the active hatred of a rival Hindú zealot, Daníchand Cshatríya, whose writings he refused to admit into the Adi-Grant'h, on the ground that the tenets inculcated in them were irreconcileable to the pure doctrine of the unity and omnipotence of God, taught in that sacred volume. This rival had sufficient influence with the Muhammedan governor of the province to procure the imprisonment of Arjun; who is affirmed, by some writers, to have died from the severity of his confinement; and, by others, to have been put to death in the most cruel manner. In whatever way his life was terminated, there can be no doubt, from its consequences, that it was considered, by his followers, as an atrocious murder, committed by the Muhammedan government; and the Sikhs, who had been, till then, an inoffensive, peaceable sect, took arms under Har Góvind, the son of Arjunmal, and wreaked their vengeance upon all whom they thought concerned in the death of their revered priest.

The contest carried on by Har Góvind against the Muhammedan chiefs in the Penjáb, though no doubt marked by that animosity which springs from a deep and implacable sense of injury on one part, and the insolence and violence of insulted power on the other, could not have been of great magnitude or importance, else it would have been more noticed by contemporary Muhammedan writers; but it was the first fruits of that desperate spirit of hostility, which was soon after to distinguish the wars between the followers of Nánac and those of Muhammed: and, from every account of Har Góvind's life, it appears to have been his anxious wish to inspire his followers with the most irreconcileable hatred of their oppressors.

It is stated, that this warlike* Gúrú, or

* Several historical accounts of the Sikhs, particularly that published by Major Browne, which is, in general, drawn from authentic sources, appear to be in error with regard to the period at which this race first took arms, which the last author states to have occurred under Gúrú Góvind; but several Sikh authors, of great respectability and information, agree in ascribing to the efforts of Har Góvind, the son of Arjun, this great change in the Sikh commonwealth; and their correctness, in this point, appears to be placed

priest militant, wore two swords in his girdle. Being asked why he did so: "The "one," said he, "is to revenge the death "of my father; the other, to destroy the "miracles of Muhammed."

beyond all question, by a passage in the Ratnávalí of B'hai Gúrú Dás B'halé; who observes, "That five phials "(of divine grace) were distributed to five Pírs (holy "men), but the sixth Pír was a mighty Gúrú (priest). "Arjun threw off his earthly frame, and the form "of Har Góvind mounted the seat of authority. The "Sóndi race continued exhibiting their different forms "in their turns. Har Góvind was the destroyer of "armies, a martial Gúrú (priest), a great warrior, and "performed great actions." The mistake of some European writers on this subject probably originated in a confusion of verbal accounts; and the similarity of the name of Har Góvind, the son of Arjunmal, and Góvínd, the last and greatest of the Sikh Gúrús, the son of Tégh Bahádur. In the Persian sketch, which Major Browne translates, the name of Har Góvind is not mentioned. The son of Arjunmal is called Gúrú Rám Ráy, which is obviously a mistake of the author of that manuscript.

Har Góvind is reputed, by some authors, to have been the first who allowed his followers to eat* the flesh of all animals, with the exception of the cow: and it appears not improbable that he made this great change in their diet at the time when he effected a still more remarkable revolution in their habits, by converting a race of peaceable enthusiasts into an intrepid band of soldiers†. He had five sons, Bábú Gúrúdaitya, Saurat Singh, Tégh Bahádur, Anna Ray, and Atal Ray. The two last died

* Nánac had forbidden hog's flesh, though a common species of food among the lower tribe of Hindús, in compliance with the prejudices of the Muhammedans, whom it was his great wish to reconcile to his faith by every concession and persuasion.

† It is stated, by a Sikh author named Nand, that Har Góvind, during his ministry, established the practice of invoking the three great Hindú deities, Brahmá, Vishnu, and Síva: but this is not confirmed by any other authority which I have seen.

without descendants. Saurat Singh and Tégh Singh, or Tégh Bahádur, were, by the cruel persecution of the Muhammedans, forced to fly into the mountains to the northward of the Penjáb. His eldest son, Gurudaítya, died early, but left two sons, Dáharmal and Har Ráy; the latter of whom succeeded his grandfather, who died in the year A. D. 1644, and of the Samvat 1701. It does not appear that Har Ráy enjoyed much temporal power, or that he entered into any hostilities with the Muhammedans: his rule was tranquil, and passed without any remarkable event; owing, probably, to the vigor which the Muhammedan power had attained in the early part of the reign of Aurungzeb. At his death, which happened in the year A. D. 1661, and of the Samvat 1718, a violent contest arose among the Sikhs, regarding the succession to the office of spiritual leader; for the temporal power of their ruler was, at this period, little more than nominal. The dispute between his sons, or, as some Sikh authors state, his son and grandson, Har Crishn and Rám Ráy, was referred to Dehli, whither both parties went; and, by an imperial decree of Aurungzeb, the Sikhs were allowed to elect their own priest. They chose Har Crishn, who died at Dehli in the year A. D. 1664, and of the Samvat 1721; and was succeeded by his uncle, Tégh Behádur. He, however, had to encounter the most violent opposition from his nephew, Rám Ráy*, who remained

* The violent contests of the Sikhs are mentioned by most of their writers; and, though they disagree in their accounts, they all represent Tégh Behádur as falling the innocent sacrifice of Muhammedan despotism and intolerance; which, from the evidence of all respectable contemporary Muhammedan authors, would appear not to be the fact. Tégh Behádur, agreeable to them, provoked his execution by a series of crimes. He joined, they state, with a Moslem Fakír, of the name of Hafiz ed Dín; and, supported by a body of armed mendicants, committed the most violent depredations on the peaceable

at Dehli, and endeavoured, by every art and intrigue, to effect his ruin: he was seized, and brought to Dehli, in consequence of his nephew's misrepresentations; and, after being in prison for two years, was released at the intercession of Jayasingh, Rájá of Jayapúr, whom he accompanied to Bengal. Tégh Behádur afterwards took up his abode at the city of Patna*; but was pursued, agreeable to Sikh authors, to his retreat, with implacable rancour, by the jealousy and ambition of Rám Ráy; who at last accomplished the destruction of his rival. He was brought from Patna, and, by the accounts of the same authors, publicly put to death, without even the allegation of a crime, beyond a firm and

inhabitants of the Penjáb. The author of the Seir Mutákhherin says he was, in consequence of these excesses, put to death at Gwalior, and his body cut into four quarters, one of which was hung up at each gate of the fortress.

* A Sikh college was founded in that city.

undaunted assertion of the truth of that faith of which he was the high priest. This event is said to have taken place in the year A. D. 1675, and of the Samvat 1732: but the Sikh records of their own history, from the death of Har Góvind to that of Tégh Behádur, are contradictory and unsatisfactory, and appear to merit little attention. The fact is, that the sect was almost crushed, in consequence of their first effort to attain power, under Har Góvind; and, from the period of his death to that of Tégh Behádur, the Mogul empire was, as has been before stated, in the zenith of its power, under Aurungzeb: and the Sikhs, who had never attained any real strength, were rendered still weaker by their own internal dissensions. Their writers have endeavoured to supply this chasm in their history by a fabulous account of the numerous miracles which were wrought by their priests, Rám Ráy, Har Crishn, and even the unfortunate Tégh Behádur, at

Dehli, all of whom are said to have astonished the emperor and his nobles, by a display of their supernatural powers: but their wide difference from each other, in these relations, would prove, if any proof was wanting, that all the annals of that period are fabricated.

The history of the Sikhs, after the death of Tégh Behádur, assumes a new aspect. It is no longer the record of a sect, who, revering the conciliatory and mild tenets of their founder, desired more to protect themselves than to injure others; but that of a nation, who, adding to a deep sense of the injuries they had sustained from a bigotted and overbearing government, all the ardour of men commencing a military career of glory, listened, with rapture, to a son glowing with vengeance against the murderers of his father, who taught a doctrine suited to the troubled state of his mind, and called upon his followers, by every feeling of manhood, to lay aside their peaceable habits, to graft the resolute courage of the soldier on the enthusiastic faith of the devotee, to swear eternal war with the cruel and haughty Muhammedans, and to devote themselves to *steel*, as the only means of obtaining every blessing that this world, or that to come, could afford to mortals.

This was the doctrine of Gúrú Góvind, the son of Tégh Behádur; who, though very young at his father's death, had his mind imbued with the deepest horror at that event, and cherished a spirit of implacable resentment against those whom he considered as his murderers. Devoting his life to this object, we find him, when quite a youth, at the head of a large party of his followers, amid the hills of Srínagar, where he gave proofs of that ardent and daring mind, which afterwards raised him to such eminence. He was not, however, able to maintain himself against the prince of that country, with whom he had entered into hostilities; and, being obliged to leave it, he went to the Penjáb, where he was warmly welcomed by a Hindú chief in rebellion against the government. This chief gave Góvind possession of Mák'havál*, and several other villages, where he settled with his followers, and repaid his benefactor by aiding him in his depredations. Góvind appears, at this moment, to have been universally acknowledged by the Sikhs, as their Sat-gúrú, or chief spiritual leader; and he used the influence which that station, his sufferings, and the popularity of his cause, gave him, to effect a complete change in the habits and religion of his countrymen†. It would be tedious and useless to follow the Sikh writers through those volumes of fables in which they have narrated the wonders that prognosticated the rise of this,

* A town on the Satléj.

† Gúrú Góvind is stated, by a Sikh author of respectability, B'hai Gúrú Dás B'halé, to have been fourteen years of age when his father was put to death.

the most revered of all their priests, to power; or to enter, at any length, into those accounts which they, and Góvind himself, for he is equally celebrated as an author and as a warrior, have given of his exploits. It will be sufficient, for the purpose of this sketch, to state the essential changes which he effected in his tribe, and the consequences of his innovations.

Though the Sikhs had already, under Har Góvind, been initiated in arms, yet they appear to have used these only in self-defence: and as every tribe of Hindús, from the Brahmen to the lowest of the Súdra, may, in cases of necessity, use them without any infringement of the original institutions of their tribe, no violation of these institutions was caused by the rules of Nánac; which, framed with a view to conciliation, carefully abstained from all interference with the civil institutes of the Hindús. But his more daring successor, Gúrú Góvind, saw that such observances were at variance with the plans of his lofty ambition; and he wisely judged, that the only means by which he could ever hope to oppose the Muhammedan government with success, were not only to admit converts from all tribes, but to break, at once, those rules by which the Hindús had been so long chained; to arm, in short, the whole population of the country, and to make worldly wealth and rank an object to which Hindús, of every class, might aspire.

The extent to which Góvind succeeded in this design will be more fully noticed in another place. It is here only necessary to state the leading features of those changes by which he subverted, in so short a time, the hoary institutions of Brahmá*, and excited

* The object of Nánac was to abolish the distinctions of cast amongst the Hindús, and to bring them to the adoration of that Supreme Being, before whom all men, he contended, were equal. Gúrú Góvind, who adopted all the principles of his celebrated predecessor, as far as religious usages were concerned, is

terror and astonishment in the minds of the Muhammedan conquerors of India, who saw the religious prejudices of the Hindús, which they had calculated upon as one of the pillars of their safety, because they limited the great majority of the population to peaceable occupations, fall before the touch of a bold and enthusiastic innovator, who opened at once, to men of the lowest tribe*, the dazzling prospect of earthly glory. All who subscribed to his tenets were upon a

reported to have said, on this subject, that the four tribes of Hindús, the Brahmen, Cshatriya, Vaisya, and Súdra, would, like *pán* (betle-leaf), *chunám* (lime), *supári* (betle-nut), and *khat* (*terra japonica*, or *catechu*), become all of one colour, when well chewed.

* Some men of the lowest Hindú tribe, of the occupation of sweepers, were employed to bring away the corpse of Tégh Béhadur from Dehli. Their success was rewarded by high rank and employment. Several of the same tribe, who have become Sikhs, have been remarkable for their valour, and have attained great reputation. They are distinguished, among the Sikhs, by the name of Ran-Rata Singh.

level, and the Brahmen who entered his sect had no higher claims to eminence than the lowest Súdra who swept his house. It was the object of Góvind to make all Sikhs equal*, and that their advancement should solely depend upon their exertions: and well aware how necessary it was to inspire men of a low race, and of groveling minds, with pride in themselves, he changed the name of his followers from Sikh to Singh, or lion; thus giving to all his followers that honourable title which had been before exclusively assumed by the Rajapúts, the first military class of Hindús: and every

* That is, equal in civil rights. He wished to remove the disqualifications of birth, and do away cast. That he did not completely effect this object, and that some distinctions of their former tribes, particularly those relating to intermarriage, should still be kept up by the Sikhs, cannot be a matter of astonishment to those acquainted with the deep-rooted prejudices of the Hindús upon this point; which is as much a feeling of family pride as of religious usage.

Sikh felt himself at once elevated to rank with the highest, by this proud appellation.

The disciples of Góvind were required to devote themselves to arms, always to have *steel* about them in some shape or other; to wear a blue dress; to allow their hair to grow; to exclaim, when they met each other, *Wá! Gúrújí ká khálsah! Wá! Gúrují ki futteh!* which means, "Success to the "state of the Gúrú! Victory attend the "Gúrú*! The intention of some of these institutions is obvious; such as that principle of devotion to *steel*, by which all were made soldiers; and that exclamation, which made the success of their priest, and that of the commonwealth, the object of their hourly prayer. It became, in fact, the watchword which was continually to revive, in the minds of the Sikh disciple, the obligations he owed to that community of

* Spiritual leader.

which he had become a member, and to that faith which he had adopted.

Of the causes which led Góvind to enjoin his followers to regard it as impious to cut the hair of their heads, or shave their beards, very different accounts are given. Several Muhammedan authors state, that both this ordination, and the one which directed his followers to wear blue clothes, was given in consequence of his gratitude to some Afghán mountaineers, who aided his escape from a fort, in which he was besieged, by clothing him in a chequered blue dress, and causing him to allow his hair to grow, in order to pass him for one of their own Pírs, or holy fathers; in which they succeeded. This account, however, is not supported by any Sikh writer; and one of the most respectable and best informed authors of that sect states, that when Gúrú Góvind first went to Anandpúr Mák'haval, which was also called Césgher, or the house of hair, he spent much of his time in devotion, at a temple of Durga Bhavaní, the goddess of courage, by whom he was directed to unloose his hair and draw his sword. Góvind, in consequence of this pretended divine order, vowed he would preserve his hair, as consecrated to that divinity, and directed his followers to do the same*. The origin of that blue chequered† dress, which was at one time worn by all Góvind's followers, and is still worn by the Acálís, or *never-dying*, (the most remarkable class of devotees of that sect,) is differently stated by different authors: but it appears probable, that both these institutions proceeded from the policy

* The goddess Durgá Bhaváni is said, by a Sikh author, to be represented, in some images, with her hair long and dishevelled.

† This institution is also said to be borrowed from the Hindú mythology. Bala Rám, the elder brother of Crishna, wore blue clothes; from which he is called Nilámbar, or *the clothed in dark blue*; and Shitivas, or *the blue clothed*.

of Góvind, who sought to separate his followers from all other classes of India, as much by their appearance as by their religion: and he judged with wisdom when he gave consequence to such distinctions; which, though first established as mere forms, soon supersede the substance of belief; and, when strengthened by usage, become the points to which ignorant and unenlightened minds have, in all ages of the world, shown the most resolute and unconquerable adherence.

Gúrú Góvind inculcated his tenets upon his followers by his preaching, his actions, and his works; among which is the Dasamá Pádsháh ka Grant'h, or the book of the tenth king or ruler; Gúrú Góvind being the tenth leader of the sect from Nánac. This volume, which is not limited to religious subjects, but filled with accounts of his own battles, and written with the view of stirring up a spirit of valour and emulation among his followers, is at least as much revered, among the Sikhs, as the Adi-Grant'h of Arjunmal. Góvind is said to have first instituted the Gúrú Mata, or state council, among the Sikhs; which meets at Amritsar. The constitution and usages of this national assembly will be described hereafter: it is here only necessary to observe, that its institution adds one more proof to those already stated, of the comprehensive and able mind of this bold reformer, who gave, by its foundation, that form of a federative republic, to the commonwealth of the Sikhs, which was most calculated to rouse his followers from their indolent habits, and deep-rooted prejudices, by giving them a personal share in the government, and placing within the reach of every individual the attainment of rank and influence in the state.

It could not be expected that Gúrú Góvind could accomplish all those great schemes he had planned. He planted the tree; but it was not permitted, according to

Sikh writers, that he should see it in that maturity which it was destined to reach: and this, these authors state, was foretold to him by some Brahmens, skilled in necromancy. It would be tedious to dwell on such fables*; and it is time to return to the

* One of the most popular of these fables states, that in the year of the Híjerah 1118, Gúrú Góvind, agreeably to the directions he had received from two Brahmen necromancers, threw a number of magical compounds, given him by these Brahmens, into a fire, near which he continued in prayers for several days. A sword of lightning at last burst from the flame of fire; but Góvind, instead of seizing this sword in an undaunted manner, as he was instructed, was dazzled by its splendour, and shrunk from it in alarm. The sword instantly flew to heaven; from whence a loud voice was heard to say, "Gúrú Góvind! thy wishes shall be fulfilled by thy posterity, "and thy followers shall daily increase." The Brahmens were in despair at this failure; but, after deep reflection, they told Góvind, there was still one mode of acquiring that honour for himself, which appeared, by the decree that had been pronounced, doomed for his posterity. If he would only allow them to take off his

political life of Góvind, which is marked by but few events of importance. These are either related by Muhammedan authors, who detract from all the pretensions of this enemy of their faith and name; by his disciples, who exalt the slightest of his actions into the achievements of a divinity; or by himself, for he wrote an account of his own wars. This last work, however, is more calculated to inflame the courage of his followers, than to convey correct information of actual events.

Gúrú Góvind Singh, in the Vichitra Nátac, a work written by himself, and inserted in the Dasama Pádsháh ka Grant'h, traces the descent of the Cshatriya tribe of Sóndí, to which he belongs, from a race of Hindú

head, and throw it into the fire, he would be resuscitated to the enjoyment of the greatest glory. The Gúrú excused himself from trying this experiment, declaring that he was content that his descendants should enjoy the fruits of that tree which he had planted.

Rájás*, who founded the cities of Casúr and Lahore. He was born, he states, at Patan, or Patna, and brought up at Madra Dés, in the Penjáb. He went, after his father's death, to the banks of the Cálíndí, or Yamuná, and addicted himself to hunting the wild beasts of the forest, and other manly diversions: but this occupation, he adds, offended the emperor of Dehli, who ordered chiefs, of the Muhammedan race, to attack him. Gúrú Góvind describes, in this work, with great animation, his own feats, and those of his friends†, in the first

* These Rájás appear, from the same authority, to be descended in a direct line from Hindú gods.

† The following short extract from the translation of the Vichitra Nátac, will show that Góvind gave his friends their full meed of praise, and will also exhibit the character of his style: "Cripál rages, wielding his "mace: he crushed the skull of the fierce Hyát "Khan. He made the blood spurt aloft, and scat-"tered the brains of the chief, as Crishna crushed the "earthen vessel of butter. Then Nand Chand raged "in dreadful ire, launching the spear, and wielding

of his actions; in which, by his account, the arrows of the Sikhs were victori-

" the sword. He broke his keen scimitar, and drew " his dagger, to support the honour of the Sóndi race. " Then my maternal uncle, Cripál, advanced in his " rage, and exhibited the skilful war-feats of a true " Cshatriya. The mighty warrior, though struck by " an arrow, with another made a valiant Khán fall " from his saddle, and Sáheb Chand, of the Cshatriya " race, strove in the battle's fury, and slew a blood- " thirsty Khán, a warrior of Khorásan." After recording the actions of many others, Góvind thus describes his own deeds: " The blood-drinking spectres and " ghosts yelled for carnage; the fierce Vetála, the " chief of the spectres, laughed for joy, and sternly " prepared for his repast. The vultures hovered " around, screaming for their prey. Hari Chand, (a " Hindú chief in the emperor's army,) in his wrath, " drawing his bow, first struck my steed with an " arrow: aiming a second time, he discharged his " arrow; but the Deity preserved me, and it passed " me, and only grazed my ear. His third arrow struck " my breast: it tore open the mail, and pierced the " skin, leaving a slight scar; but the God whom I " adore saved me. When I felt this hurt, my anger " was kindled; I drew my bow and discharged an

ous over the sabres of the Muhammedans *.

This first success appears to have greatly increased the number of Gúrú Góvind's followers, whom he established at Anandpúr, Khílór, and the towns in their vicinity; where they remained, till called to

" arrow: all my champions did the same, rushing " onwards to the battle. Then I aimed at the young " hero, and struck him. Hari Chand perished, and " many of his host; death devoured him, who was " called a Rájá among a hundred thousand Rájás. " Then all the host, struck with consternation, fled, " deserting the field of combat. I obtained the vic" tory through the favour of the Most High; and, " victorious in the field, we raised aloud the song of " triumph. Riches fell on us like rain, and all our " warriors were glad."

* Hyát Khan and Nejábet Khán are mentioned as two of the principal chiefs of the emperor's army that fell in this first action. Góvind, speaking of the fall of the latter, says: " When Nejábet Khán fell, the " world exclaimed, Alas! but the region of Swarga " (the heavens) shouted victory."

aid the Rájá of Nadón*, Bhíma Chand, who was threatened with an invasion by the Rájá of Jammu; who had been excited to hostilities by Mía Khan, a Mogul chief, then at war with Bhíma Chand.

Gúrú Góvind gives an account of this war, which consisted of attacking and defending the narrow passes of the mountains. He describes Bhíma Chand and himself as leading on their warriors, who advanced, he says, to battle, "like a stream "of flame consuming the forest." They were completely successful in this expedition; the Rájá of Jammu, and his Mu-

* A mountainous tract of country, that borders on the Penjáb. It lies to the N. W. of Srínagar, and the S. E. of Jammu. The present Rájá, Sansár Chand, is a chief of great respectability. His country has lately been overrun by the Rájá of Nepál and Gorc'ha. I derived considerable information regarding this family, and their territories, from the envoy of Sansár Chand, who attended Lord Lake, in 1805, when the British army was in the Penjáb.

hammedan allies, having been defeated, and chased with disgrace across the Satléj.

Gúrú Góvind next relates the advance of the son of Diláwer Khán against him. The object of the Muhammedan chief appears to have been, to surprise Góvind and his followers at night: but, when that project was defeated, his troops were seized with a panic, and fled from the Sikhs without a contest. The father, enraged at the disgraceful retreat of his son, collected all his followers, and sent Husain Khán, who made successful inroads upon the Sikhs, taking several of their principal forts*. A

* Though the account of this war is given in a style sufficiently inflated for the wars of the demons and angels; yet, as Góvind relates, that Husain Khán returned a messenger, which one of the principal Rájás had sent him, with this message to his master; "Pay "down ten thousand rupees, or destruction descends "on thy head;" we may judge, both from the demand, and the amount of the contribution, of the nature of this contest, as well as its scale. It was evidently one of those petty provincial wars, which took place in

general action at last took place, in which the Khán, after performing prodigies of valour, was defeated, and lost his life. Gúrú Góvind was not present at this battle. "The lord of the earth," he says, "detained me from this conflict, and caused "the rain of steel to descend in another "quarter."

Diláwer Khán and Rustam Khán next marched against the Sikhs, who appear to have been disheartened at the loss of some of their principal chiefs, and more at the accounts they received of Aurungzeb's rage at their progress, and of his having detached his son to the district of Madra*,

every remote part of the Indian empire, when it was distracted: and, at this period, Aurungzeb was wholly engaged in the Dek'hin, and the northern provinces were consequently neglected, and their governments in a weak and unsettled state.

* This must have been in the year 1701, when Baháder Shah was detached from the Dek'hin to take charge of the government of Cábul, and was probably ordered, at the same time, to settle the disturbances in the Penjáb.

in order to take measures to quell them. At the prince's approach, " every body," says Gúrú Góvind, " was struck with terror. " Unable to comprehend the ways of the " Eternal, several deserted me, and fled, " and took refuge in the lofty mountains. " These vile cowards were," he adds, " too " greatly alarmed in mind to understand " their own advantage; for the emperor " sent troops, who burnt the habitations of " those that had fled." He takes this occasion of denouncing every misery that this world can bring, and all the pains and horrors of the next, on those who desert their Gúrú, or priest. " The man who " does this," he writes, " shall neither have " child nor offspring. His aged parents " shall die in grief and sorrow, and he " shall perish like a dog, and be thrown " into hell to lament." After many more curses on apostates, he concludes this anathema by stating, that the good genius of prosperity in this world, and eternal blessings in the next, shall be the certain reward of all who remain attached to their Gúrú: and, as an instance, he affirms, that not one of those faithful followers, who had adhered to him at this trying crisis, had received the least injury*.

Gúrú Góvind closes his first work, the Vichitra Nátac, with a further representation on the shame that attends apostasy, and the rewards that await those that prove true to their religion; and he concludes by a prayer to the Deity, and a declaration of his intention to compose, for the use of his disciples, a still larger work; by which

* There is a remarkable passage in this chapter, in which Gúrú Góvind appears to acknowledge the supremacy of the emperor. "God," he says, "formed "both Baba (Nánac) and Báber (the emperor of that "name). Look upon Baba as the Padshah (king) of "religion, and Báber, the lord of the world. He "who will not give Nánac a single damri, (a coin the "sixteenth part of an ana,) will receive a severe "punishment from Báber."

the Sikhs conceive that he meant the rest of the Dasama Pádsháh ka Grant'h, of which the Vichitra Nátac forms the first section.

An account of Góvind's war with the Rájá of Kahilúr*, is found in a work written in the Dúgar, or mountain dialect of the Penjábi tongue, which gives an account of some other actions of this chief. Though this account is greatly exaggerated, it no doubt states some facts correctly, and therefore merits a brief notice. According to this authority, the Rájás of Kahilúr, Jiswál, and others, being defeated and disgraced in several actions, applied to the court of Aurungzéb for aid against Gúrú Góvind, from whom they stated that they had received great injuries. When the emperor

* Kahilúr, or Kahlóre, is situated on the Satléj, above Mák'havál. It is near the mountains through which that river flows into the Penjáb. Another place of the name of Kahlúr, or Kahlóre, is situated a short distance from Lahore, to the N. E. of that city.

asked who made the complaint, the answer was: "It is the chief of Kahilur, thy "servant, who has been despoiled of his "country by violence, though a faithful "Zemindar (landholder), and one who has "always been punctual in paying his con-"tributions." Such were the representations, this author states, by which they obtained the aid of an army from the emperor.

Their combined forces proceeded against Gúrú Góvind and his followers, who were obliged to shut themselves up in their fortresses, where they endured every misery that sickness and famine can bring upon a besieged place. Góvind, after suffering the greatest hardships, determined to attempt his escape. He ordered his followers to leave the fort, one by one, at midnight, and to separate the moment they went out. The misery of this separation, which divided the father from the child, the husband from the wife, and brothers from sisters, was horrible; but it was the only chance which they had of safety, and his orders were obeyed. He himself went, among the rest; and, after undergoing great fatigue, and escaping many dangers, he arrived at Chamkóur, by the Rájá of which place he was received in a kind and friendly manner. His enemies had entered the fortress which Góvind left, the moment he fled, and made many prisoners; among which were his mother and his two children, who were carried to Foujdar Khán, the governor of Sirhind, by whose orders they were inhumanly massacred*. The army of the emperor, aided by the Rájás hostile to Góvind, next marched to Chamkóur, and encompassed it on all sides. Góvind, in despair, clasping his hands, called upon the goddess of the sword†. "The world sees," he exclaimed,

* The Muhammedan authors blame Vízír Khán for this unnecessary and impolitic act of barbarity.

† Bhaváni Durgá.

"that we have no help but thee!" saying which, he prepared, with his few followers, to make the most desperate resistance.

The emperor's army, employed at this period against Góvind, was commanded by Khwájeh Muhammed and Nahar Khán, who deputed, at the commencement of the siege, an envoy to the Sikh leader, with the following message: "This army is not one "belonging to Rájás and Ránás: it is that "of the great Aurungzeb: show, therefore, "thy respect, and embrace the true faith." The envoy proceeded, in the execution of his mission, with all the pride of those he represented. "Listen," said he, from himself to Gúrú Góvind, "to the words of the "Nawáb: leave off contending with us, "and playing the infidel; for it is evident "you never can reap advantage from such "an unequal war." He was stopped by Ajit Singh, the son of Góvind, from saying more. That youth, seizing his scimetar, exclaimed: "If you utter another word, I

" will humble your pride: I will smite " your head from your body, and cut you " to pieces, for daring to speak such lan- " guage before our chiefs." The blood of the envoy boiled with rage, and he returned with this answer to his master.

This effort to subdue the fortitude and faith of Góvind having failed, the siege commenced with great vigour. A long description is given by B'hai Gúrú Dás B'halé and other Sikh authors, of the actions that were performed. Amongst the most distinguished, were those of the brave, but unfortunate, Ajit Singh*, the son of

* In the Penjábi narrative of B'hai Gúrú Dás B'halé, the actions of Ajit Singh, and Ranjit Singh, sons of Góvind, are particularly described; and, from one part of the description, it would appear that the family of Góvind, proud of their descent, had not laid aside the *zunár*, or holy cord, to which they were, as belonging to the Cshatriya race, entitled. Speaking of these youths, the author says: " Slaughtering every " Turk and Pahlan whom they saw, they adorned

Gúrú Góvind, whose death is thus recorded: "A second time the Khán advanced, and "the battle raged. Some fought, some "fled. Ajit Singh, covered with glory, "departed to Swarga (heaven). Indra*, "first of the gods (Dévatás), advanced "with the celestial host to meet him; he "conducted him to Dévapúr, the city of "the gods, and seated him on a celestial "throne: having remained there a short "time, he proceeded to the region of the "sun. Thus," he concludes, "Ajit Singh "departed in glory; and his fame extends

"their sacred strings, by converting them into sword-"belts. Returning from the field, they sought their "father, who bestowed a hundred blessings on their "scimetars."

* The Sikh author, though he may reject the superstitious idolatry of the Hindús, adorns his descriptions with every image its mythology can furnish; and claims for his hero the same high honours in Swarga, that a Brahmen would expect for one of the Pándu race.

" over three worlds, for the fame of the
" warrior lives for ever."

Though Góvind showed an invincible spirit, and performed prodigies of valour, having killed, with his own hand, Nahar Khán, and wounded Khwájeh Muhammed, the other leader of the emperor's troops, it was impossible to contend longer against such superior numbers; and he at last, taking advantage of a dark night, fled from Chamkóur, covering his face, according to the Sikh author, from shame at his own disgrace.

This sketch of the life of Góvind is compiled from his own works, and those of other Sikh writers, such as Nand and B'hai Gúrú Dás; and the events recorded, allowing for the colouring with which such narratives are written in the East, appear to be correct: the leading facts are almost all established by the evidence of contemporary Muhammedan writers, to whom we must trust for the remainder of his history; as the authorities we have followed end at the period of his flight from Chamkóur.

Most accounts agree that Gúrú Góvind, after his flight, was, from a sense of his misfortunes, and the loss of his children, bereft of his reason, and wandered about for a considerable time in the most deplorable condition. One account states, that he died in the Penjáb; another, that he went to Patna, where he ended his days; a third, taken from a Sikh authority*, asserts that Gúrú Góvind, after remaining some time in the Lak'hi-Jungle, to which he had fled, returned without molestation

* Mr. Foster has followed this authority in his account of the Sikh nation: and I am inclined to believe that the part of it which relates to Gúrú Góvind's dying at Nadér, in the Dek'hin, of a wound received from a Patán, is correct; as it is written on the last page of a copy of the Adi-Grant'h, in my possession, with several other facts relative to the dates of the births and deaths of the principal high priests of the Sikhs.

to his former residence in the Penjáb; and that, so far from meeting with any persecution from the Muhammedan government, he received favours from the emperor, Bahâder Sháh; who, aware of his military talents, gave him a small military command in the Dek'hin, where he was stabbed by a Patán soldier's son, and expired of his wounds, in the year 1708, at Nadér, a town situate on the Godaveri river, about one hundred miles from Haiderabad.

It is sufficiently established, from these contradictory and imperfect accounts of the latter years of Gúrú Góvind, that he performed no actions worthy of record after his flight from Chamkóur: and when we consider the enthusiastic ardour of his mind, his active habits, his valour, and the insatiable thirst of revenge, which he had cherished through life, against the murderers of his father, and the oppressors of his sect, we cannot think, when that leading passion of his mind must have been increased by the massacre of his children, and the death or mutilation* of his most attached followers, that he would have remained inactive; much less that he would have sunk into a servant of that government, against which he had been in constant rebellion: nor is it likely that such a leader as Gúrú Góvind could ever have been trusted by a Muhammedan prince: and there appears, therefore, every reason to give credit to those accounts which state, that mental distraction, in consequence of deep distress and disappointment, was the cause of the inactivity of Gúrú Góvind's declining years. Nor is such a conclusion at all at variance with the fact of his being killed at Nadér, as it is probable, even if he was reduced to the state described, that he continued, till the close of his existence,

* Both at Chamkóur, and other forts, from which the famished Sikhs attempted to escape, many of them were taken, and had their noses and ears cut off.

that wandering and adventurous life to which he had been so early accustomed.

In the character of this reformer of the Sikhs, it is impossible not to recognise many of those features which have distinguished the most celebrated founders of political communities. The object he attempted was great and laudable. It was the emancipation of his tribe from oppression and persecution; and the means which he adopted, were such as a comprehensive mind could alone have suggested. The Muhammedan conquerors of India, as they added to their territories, added to their strength, by making proselytes through the double means of persuasion and force; and these, the moment they had adopted their faith, became the supporters of their power against the efforts of the Hindús; who, bound in the chains of their civil and religious institutions, could neither add to their number by admitting converts, nor allow more than a small proportion of the population of the country to arm against the enemy. Góvind saw that he could only hope for success by a bold departure from usages which were calculated to keep those, by whom they were observed, in a degraded subjection to an insulting and intolerant race. "You make Hindús Mu-"hammedans, and are justified by your "laws," he is said to have written to Aurungzeb: "now I, on a principle of self-"preservation, which is superior to all "laws, will make Muhammedans Hindús*. "You may rest," he added, "in fancied "security: but beware! for I will teach "the sparrow to strike the eagle to the "ground." A fine allusion to his design of

* Meaning Sikhs; whose faith, though it differs widely from the present worship of the Hindús, has been thought to have considerable analogy to the pure and simple religion originally followed by that nation.

inspiring the lowest races among the Hindús with that valour and ambition which would lead them to perform the greatest actions.

The manner in which Góvind endeavoured to accomplish the great plan he had formed, has been exhibited in the imperfect sketch given of his life. His efforts to establish that temporal power in his own person, of which he laid the foundation for his tribe, were daring and successful in as great a degree as circumstances would admit: but it was not possible he could create means, in a few years, to oppose, with success, the force of one of the greatest empires in the universe. The spirit, however, which he infused into his followers, was handed down as a rich inheritance to their children; who, though they consider Bábá Nánác as the author of their religion, revere, with a just gratitude, Gúrú Góvind, as the founder of their worldly greatness and political independence. They are conscious, indeed, that they have become, from the adoption of his laws and institutions, the scourge of their enemies; and have conquered and held, for more than half a century, the finest portion of the once great empire of the house of Taimur.

Gúrú Góvind was the last acknowledged religious ruler of the Sikhs. A prophecy had limited their spiritual guides to the number of ten; and their superstition, aided, no doubt, by the action of that spirit of independence which his institutions had introduced, caused its fulfilment. The success, however, of Banda, a Bairági, who was the devoted follower and friend of Gúrú Góvind, established their union under his banners. A short period after Góvind's death, the grief of Banda at the misfortune of his priest, is said, by Sikh authors, to have settled into a gloomy and desperate desire to revenge his wrongs. The confusion which took place on the death of Aurungzeb, which happened in the year 1707, was favourable to his wishes. After plundering the country, and defeating most of the petty Muhammedan chiefs that were opposed to him, he thought himself sufficiently strong to venture on an action with Foujdar Khán, the governor of the province of Sarhind, and the man of all others most abhorred by the Sikhs, as the murderer of the infant children of Gúrú Góvind. This action was fought with valour by the Muhammedans; and with all that desperation on the part of the Sikhs, which the most savage spirit of revenge could inspire: and this, aided by the courage and conduct of their leader, gave them the victory, after a severe contest. Foujdar Khán fell, with most of his army, to whom the enraged Sikhs gave no quarter. Nor was their savage revenge satiated by the destruction of the Muhammedan army: they put to death the wife and children of Vizír Khán, and almost all the inhabitants of Sarhind. They destroyed or polluted the mosques of that city; and, in a spirit of wild and brutal rage, dug up the carcasses of the dead, and exposed them to be devoured by beasts of prey. Encouraged by this success, and hardened by the lessons of Banda to deeds of the most horrid atrocity, the Sikhs rushed forward, and subdued all the country between the Satléj and the Jumna; and, crossing that river, made inroads into the province of Sáháranpúr*. It is unnecessary to state the particulars of this memorable incursion, which, from all accounts, appears to have been one of the severest scourges with which a country was ever afflicted. Every excess that the most wanton barbarity could commit, every cruelty that an unappeased appetite of revenge could suggest, was inflicted upon the miserable inhabitants of the provinces through which they passed. Life was only granted to those who con-

* This province lies a few miles to the N. E. of Dehli, between the rivers Jumna and Ganges.

formed to the religion, and adopted the habits and dress of the Sikhs; and if Behádur Shah had not quitted the Dek'hin, which he did in A. D. 1710, there is reason to think the whole of Hindustan would have been subdued by these merciless invaders.

The first check the Sikhs received was from an army under Sultán Kúli Khán. That chief defeated one of their advanced corps at Pánipat'h, which, after being dispersed, fled to join their leader Banda, at Sarhind. The death of Behádur Shah prevented this success from being pursued; and the confusion which followed that event, was favourable to the Sikhs. Banda defeated Islám Khán, the viceroy of Lahore, and one of his fanatic followers stabbed Báyezíd Khán, the governor of Sarhind, who had marched out of that town to encounter this army. This, however, was the last of Banda's successful atrocities. Abdal Sámad Khán, a general of great reputation, was detached, with a large army, by the emperor Farakhseir, against the Sikhs, whom he defeated in a very desperate action; in which, agreeable to Muhammedan authors, Banda performed prodigies of valour, and was only obliged to give way to the superior numbers and discipline of the imperialists. The Sikhs were never able to make a stand after this defeat, and were hunted, like wild beasts, from one strong hold to another, by the army of the emperor; by whom their leader, and his most devoted followers, were at last taken, after having suffered every extreme of hunger and fatigue*.

Abdal Sámad Khán put to death great

* They were taken in the fort of Lóhgad, which is one hundred miles to the north-east of Lahore. This fortress was completely surrounded, and the Sikhs were only starved into surrender, having been reduced to such extremes, that they were reported to have eaten, what to them must have been most horrible, the flesh of the cow.

numbers of the Sikhs after the surrender of Lóhgad, the fortress in which they took refuge; but sent Banda, and the principal chiefs of the tribe, to Dehli, where they were first treated with every kind of obloquy and insult, and then executed. A Muhammedan writer* relates the intrepidity with which these Sikh prisoners, but particularly their leader, Banda, met death. "It is singular," he writes, "that these "people not only behaved firmly during "the execution, but they would dispute "and wrangle with each other who should "suffer first; and they made interest with "the executioner to obtain the preference. "Banda," he continues, "was at last pro-"duced, his son being seated in his lap. "His father was ordered to cut his throat, "which he did, without uttering one word. "Being then brought nearer the magis-

* The author of the *Seir Mutákherin*.

"trate's tribunal, the latter ordered his "flesh to be torn off with red hot pincers; "and it was in those moments he expired: "his black soul taking its flight, by one of "those wounds, towards the regions for "which it was so well fitted."

Thus perished Banda; who, though a brave and able leader, was one of the most cruel and ferocious of men, and endeavoured to impart to his followers that feeling of merciless resentment which he cherished against the whole Muhammedan race, whom he appears to have thought accountable for the cruelty and oppression of a few individuals of the persuasion*.

* It is necessary, however, to state, that there is a schismatical sect of Sikhs, who are termed Bandái, or the followers of Banda, who totally deny this account of the death of Banda, and maintain that he escaped severely wounded from his last battle, and took refuge in B'habar, where he quietly ended his days, leaving two sons, Ajit Singh and Zoráwer Singh, who success-

Though the Sikhs, from being animated by a similar feeling, and encouraged by his first successes, followed Banda to the field, they do not revere his memory; and he is termed, by some of their authors, a heretic; who, intoxicated with victory, endeavoured to change the religious institutions and laws of Gúrú Góvind, many of whose most devoted followers this fierce chief put to death, because they refused to depart from those usages which that revered spiritual leader had taught them to consider sacred. Among other changes, Banda wished to make the Sikhs abandon their blue dress, to refrain from drinking and eating flesh; and, instead of exclaiming *Wá! Gúrúji ki Futteh! Wá! Khálsaji ki Futteh!* the salutations directed by Góvind, he directed them to exclaim, *Futteh*

fully propagated his doctrine. This sect chiefly resides in Multán, Tata, and the other cities on the banks of the Indus. They receive the Adi-Grant'h, but not the Dasama Pádsháh ka Grant'h.

D'herm! Futteh dersan! which means, "Success to piety! Success to the sect!" These innovations were very generally resisted; but the dreaded severity of Banda made many conform to his orders. The class of Acálís*, or immortals, who had been established by Gúrú Góvind, continued to oppose the innovations with great obstinacy; and many of them suffered martyrdom, rather than change either their mode of salutation, diet, or dress; and, at the death of Banda, their cause triumphed. All the institutions of Gúrú Góvind were restored: but the blue dress, instead of being, as at first, worn by all, appears, from that date, to have become the particular right of the Acálís, whose valour, in its defence, well merited the exclusive privilege of wearing this original uniform of a true Sikh.

* An account of this class of Sikhs will be hereafter given.

After the defeat and death of Banda, every measure was taken, that an active resentment could suggest, not only to destroy the power, but to extirpate the race, of the Sikhs. An astonishing number of that sect must have fallen, in the last two or three years of the contest with the imperial armies, as the irritated Muhammedans gave them no quarter. After the execution of their chief, a royal edict was issued, ordering all who professed the religion of Nánac to be taken and put to death, wherever found. To give effect to this mandate, a reward was offered for the head of every Sikh; and all Hindús were ordered to shave their hair off, under pain of death. The few Sikhs, that escaped this general execution, fled into the mountains to the N. E. of the Penjáb, where they found a refuge from the rigorous persecution by which their tribe was pursued; while numbers bent before the tempest which they could not resist, and abandoning the outward usages of their religion, satisfied their consciences with the secret practice of its rites.

From the defeat and death of Banda till the invasion of India by Nádir Shah, a period of nearly thirty years, we hear nothing of the Sikhs; but, on the occurrence of that event, they are stated to have fallen upon the peaceable inhabitants of the Penjáb, who sought shelter in the hills, and to have plundered them of that property which they were endeavouring to secure from the rapacity of the Persian invader.

Enriched with these spoils, the Sikhs left the hills, and built the fort of Dalewál, on the Rávi, from whence they made predatory incursions, and are stated to have added both to their wealth and reputation, by harassing and plundering the rear of Nadir Shah's army, which, when it returned to Persia, was encumbered with spoil, and marched, from a contempt of its enemies, with a disregard to all order.

The weak state to which the empire of Hindustan was reduced; and the confusion into which the provinces of Lahore and Cábul were thrown, by the death of Nádir; were events of too favourable a nature to the Sikhs to be neglected by that race, who became daily more bold, from their numbers being greatly increased by the union of all those who had taken shelter in the mountains; the readmission into the sect of those who, to save their lives, had abjured, for a period, their usages; and the conversion of a number of proselytes, who hastened to join a standard, under which robbery was made sacred; and to plunder, was to be pious.

Aided with these recruits, the Sikhs now extended their irruptions over most of the provinces of the Penjáb: and though it was some time before they repossessed themselves of Amritsar, they began, immediately after they quitted their fastnesses, to flock to that holy city at the periods of their feasts. Some performed this pilgrimage in secret, and in disguise: but in general, according to a contemporary Muhammedan author, the Sikh horsemen were seen riding, at full gallop, towards "their favourite "shrine of devotion. They were often "slain in making this attempt, and sometimes taken prisoners; but they used, on "such occasions, to seek, instead of avoiding, the crown of martyrdom: and the "same authority states, that an instance "was never known of a Sikh, taken in his "way to Amritsar, consenting to abjure his "faith."

It is foreign to the object of this sketch to enter into a detail of those efforts by which the Sikhs rose into that power which they now possess. It will be sufficient to glance at the principal events which have marked their progress, from the period of their emerging from the mountains, to which they had been driven after the death of Banda, to that of the conquest and subjection of those fine provinces over which their rule is now established. This sect, as has been before stated, have never admitted a spiritual leader since the death of Gúrú Góvind. It was success, and the force of a savage but strong genius, which united them, for a period, under Banda; and they have, since his death, had no acknowledged general, leader, or prince. Each individual followed to the field the Sirdar or chief, who, from birth, the possession of property, or from valour and experience, had become his superior. These chiefs again were of different rank and pretensions: a greater number of followers, higher reputation, the possession of wealth, or lands, constituted that difference; and, from one or other of these causes, one chief generally enjoyed a decided pre-eminence, and, consequently, had a lead in their military councils. But, nevertheless, they always went through the form of selecting a military leader at their Gúrú-matá, or national council; where, however, influence prevailed, and the most powerful was certain of being elected.

Such a mode of government was in itself little calculated to give that strength and union which the cause of the Sikhs required: but the peculiarities of their usages, the ardent character of their faith, the power of their enemies, and the oppression they endured, amply supplied the place of all other ordinances. To unite and to act in one body, and on one principle, was, with the first Sikhs, a law of necessity: it was, amid the dangers with which they were surrounded, their only hope of success, and their sole means of preservation: and it was to these causes, combined with the weakness and internal contests of their enemies, to which this sect owes its extraordinary rise,—not to their boasted constitution; which, whether we call it an oligarchy, which it really is; or a theocracy, which the Sikhs consider it; has not a principle in its composition that would preserve it one day from ruin, if vigorously assailed. But of this their history will furnish the best example.

Encouraged by the confusion which took place on the first Afghán* invasion, the Sikhs made themselves masters of a considerable part of the Duáb of Rávi and Jalendra†, and extended their incursions to the neighbouring countries. They, however, at this period received several severe checks from Mír Manu, the governor of Lahore, who is said, by Muhammedan authors, to have been only withheld from destroying them by the counsel of his minister, Kodá Mal, who was himself a Sikh of the Khalása‡ tribe. Mír Manu

* A. D. 1746.

† The country between the rivers Raví and Béyah, and that river and the Satléj.

‡ A sect of non-conformist Sikhs, who believe in the Adi-Grant'h of Nánac, but do not conform to the institutions of Gúrú Góvind. They are called Khalása. This word is said, by some, to be from *khális, pure* or

appointed Adína Bég Khán to the charge of the countries in which the Sikhs maintained themselves; and, as that able but artful chief considered this turbulent tribe in no other light than as the means of his personal advancement, he was careful not to reduce them altogether; but, after defeating them in an action, which was fought near Mak'havál, he entered into a secret understanding with them, by which, though their excursions were limited, they enjoyed a security to which they had been unaccustomed, and from which they gathered strength and resources for future efforts.

At the death of Mír Manu*, the Sikhs took all those advantages, which the local distractions of a falling empire offered them, of extending and establishing their power.

select, and to mean the purest, or the select: by others, from *khalás*, *free*, and to mean the freed or exempt, alluding to the tribe being exempt from the usages imposed on the other Sikhs.

* A. D. 1752.

Their bands, under their most active leaders, plundered in every direction, and were successful in obtaining possession of several countries, from which they have never since been expelled: and their success, at this period, was promoted, instead of being checked, by the appointment of their old friend, Adína Bég Khán, to Lahore; as that brave chief, anxious to defend his own government against the Afgháns, immediately entered into a confederacy with the Sikhs, whom he encouraged to plunder the territories of Ahmed Shah Abdáli.

The Afghán monarch, resenting this predatory warfare, in which the governor of Lahore was supported by the court of Dehli, determined upon invading India. Adína Bég, unable to oppose him, fled; and the Sikhs could only venture to plunder the baggage, and cut off the stragglers of the Afghán army; by which they so irritated Ahmed Shah, that he threatened them with punishment on his return; and, when he marched to Cábul, he left his son, Taimur Khán, and his vizír, Jehán Khán, at Lahore, with orders to take vengeance on the Sikhs for all the excesses which they had committed. The first expedition of Taimur Khán was against their capital, Amritsar, which he destroyed, filling up their sacred tank, and polluting all their places of worship: by which action he provoked the whole race to such a degree, that they all assembled at Lahore, and not only attempted to cut off the communication between the fort and country, but collected and divided the revenues of the towns and villages around it. Taimur Khán, enraged at this presumption, made several attacks upon them, but was constantly defeated; and being at last reduced to the necessity of evacuating Lahore, and retreating to Cábul, the Sikhs, under one of their celebrated leaders, called Jasa Singh Calál, immediately took possession of the vacant Subah of Lahore, and ordered rupees to be

coined, with an inscription to the following import: "Coined by the grace of Khál-
"sah jí, in the country of Ahmed, con-
"quered by Jasa Singh Calál."

The Sikhs, who were so deeply indebted to the forbearance of Adína Bég Khán, now considered themselves above the power of that chief; who, in order to regain his government from them and the Afghāns, was obliged to invite the Mahráta leaders, Raghunát'h Ráo, Saheb Pateil, and Malhár Ráo, to enter the Penjáb. Aided by these chiefs, he first advanced to Sarhind, where he was joined by some Sikhs that remained attached to him. Samad Khán, the officer who had been left in charge of Sarhind by Ahmed Khán, found himself obliged to evacuate that place; which he had no sooner done, than the Sikhs began to plunder. The Mahrátas, always jealous of their booty, determined to attack and punish them for this violation of what they deemed their exclusive privilege: but Adína Bég receiving intelligence of their intentions, communicated it to the Sikhs; who, taking advantage of the darkness of the night, saved themselves by flight.

After the fall of Sarhind, the Mahrátas, accompanied by Adína Bég Khán, advanced to Lahore, and soon expelled both the Sikhs and the Afgháns from the principal towns of the provinces of Sarhind and Lahore; of which they not only took possession, but sent a governor to the province of Multán; and Saheb Patcil advanced to the Attock*, where he remained for a few months. But the commotions of Hindústán and the Dek'hin soon obliged these foreigners to abandon the Penjáb; which they did the same year they had reduced it. They appointed Adína Bég Khán governor of Lahore. He died in the ensuing

* The empire of the Mahrátas had, at this proud moment, reached its zenith. The battle of Pánipat'h took place soon afterwards; since which it has rapidly declined.

year; and, by his death, afforded an opportunity to the Sikhs, which they eagerly seized, to make themselves again masters of the province of Lahore. Their success was, however, soon checked by Ahmed Shah Abdáli; who, irritated by their unsubdued turbulence, and obstinate intrepidity, made every effort (after he had gained the victory of Pánipat'h, which established his supremacy at Dehli) to destroy their power; and, with this view, he entered the Penjáb early in 1762, and overran the whole of that country with a numerous army, defeating and dispersing the Sikhs in every direction. That sect, unable to make any stand against the army of the Abdáli, pursued their old plan of retreating near the mountains; and collected a large force in the northern districts of Sarhind, a distance of above one hundred miles from Lahore, where the army of Ahmed Shah was encamped. Here they conceived themselves to be in perfect safety: but that prince made one of those rapid movements for which he was so celebrated, and reaching the Sikh army on the second day, completely surprised, and defeated it with great slaughter. In this action, which was fought in February, 1762, the Sikhs are said to have lost upwards of twenty thousand men, and the remainder fled into the hills, abandoning all the lower countries to the Afghâns, who committed every ravage that a barbarous and savage enemy could devise. Amritsar was razed to the ground, and the sacred reservoir again choaked with its ruins. Pyramids* were erected, and covered with the heads of slaughtered Sikhs: and it is mentioned, that Ahmed Shah caused the walls of those mosques, which the Sikhs had polluted, to be washed with their blood,

* This is a very common usage amongst eastern conquerors. The history of Jénghíz Khán, Taimur and Nádir Shah, afford many examples of this mode of treating their vanquished enemies.

that the contamination might be removed, and the insult offered to the religion of Muhammed expiated*.

This species of savage retaliation appears to have animated, instead of depressing, the courage of the Sikhs; who, though they could not venture to meet Ahmed Shah's army in action, harassed it with an incessant predatory warfare; and, when that sovereign was obliged, by the commotions of Afghánistan, to return to Cábul, they attacked and defeated the general he had left in Lahore, and made themselves masters of that city, in which they levelled with the ground those mosques which the Afgháns had, a few months before, purified with the blood of their brethren.

Ahmed Shah, in 1763, retook Lahore, and plundered the provinces around it; but, being obliged to return to his own country in the ensuing year, the Sikhs again expelled his

* Foster's Travels, Vol. I. p. 279.

garrison, and made themselves masters of the Penjáb; and, from that period until his death, a constant war was maintained, in which the enterprise and courage of the Afghâns gradually gave way before the astonishing activity and invincible perseverance of their enemies; who, if unable to stand a general action, retreated to impenetrable mountains, and the moment they saw an advantage, rushed again into the plains with renewed vigour, and recruited numbers. Several Sikh authors, treating of the events of this period, mention a great action having been fought, by their countrymen, near Amritsar, against the whole Afghán army, commanded by Ahmed Shah in person; but they differ with regard to the date of this battle, some fixing it in 1762, and others later. They pretend that the Sikhs, inspired by the sacredness of the ground on which this action was fought, contended for victory against superior numbers with the most desperate fury, and that the battle terminated in both parties quitting the field, without either being able to claim the least advantage. The historians of Ahmed Shah are, however, silent regarding this action; which, indeed, from all the events of his long contests with the Sikhs, appears unlikely to have occurred. It is possible the Sikhs fought, at Amritsar, with a division of the Afghán army, and that might have been commanded by the prince; but it is very improbable they had ever force to encounter the concentrated army of the Abdális; before which, while it remained in a body, they appear, from the first to the last of their contests with that prince, to have always retreated, or rather fled.

The internal state of Afghánistan, since the death of Ahmed Shah, has prevented the progress of the Sikh nation receiving any serious check from that quarter; and the distracted and powerless condition of the empire of India has offered province after province to their usurpation. Their history, during this latter period, affords little but a relation of village warfare, and predatory incursions. Their hostilities were first directed against the numerous Muhammedan chiefs who were settled in the Penjáb, and who defended, as long as they could, their jágírs, or estates, against them: but these have either been conquered, or reduced to such narrow limits, as to owe their security to their insignificance, or the precarious friendship of some powerful Sikh chief, whose support they have gained; and who, by protecting them against the other leaders of his tribe, obtains a slight accession of strength and influence.

The Sikh nation, who have, throughout their early history, always appeared, like a suppressed flame, to rise into higher splendour from every attempt to crush them, had become, while they were oppressed, as formidable for their union, as for their determined courage and unconquerable spirit of resistance: but a state of persecution and distress was the one most favourable for the action of a constitution like theirs; which, formed upon general and abstract principles, required constant and great sacrifices of personal advantage to the public good; and such can alone be expected from men, acting under the influence of that enthusiasm, which the fervor of a new religion, or a struggle for independence, can alone impart, and which are ever most readily made, when it becomes obvious to all, that a complete union in the general cause is the only hope of individual safety.

The Sikhs would appear, from their own historians, to have attributed the conquests they made entirely to their valour, and to have altogether forgot that they owed them chiefly to the decline of the house of Taimúr, and the dissensions of the government of Cábul. Intoxicated with their success, they have given way to all those passions which assail the minds of men in the possession of power. The desire, which every petty chief entertained, of increasing his territories, of building strong forts, and adding to the numbers of his troops, involved them in internal wars; and these, however commenced, soon communicated to numbers, who engaged in the dispute as passion or interest dictated. Though such feuds have, no doubt, helped to maintain their military spirit, yet their extent and virulence have completely broken down that union, which their great legislator, Góvind, laboured to establish. Quarrels have been transmitted from father to son; and, in a country where the infant is devoted to *steel*, and taught to consider war as his only occupation, these could not but multiply in an extraordinary degree; and, independent of the comparative large conquests in which the greater chiefs occasionally engaged, every village* has become an object of dispute; and there are few, if any, in the Penjáb, the rule of which is not contested between brothers or near relations†. In such a state, it is obvious, the Sikhs could alone be formidable to the most weak and distracted governments. Such, indeed, was the character, till within a very late period, of all their neighbours; and they continued to plunder, with im-

* All the villages in the Penjáb are walled round; as they are in almost all the countries of India that are exposed to sudden incursions of horse, which this defence can always repel.

† When the British and Máhráta armies entered the Penjáb, they were both daily joined by discontented petty chiefs of the Sikhs, who offered their aid to the power that would put them in the possession of a village or a fort, from which, agreeably to their statement, they had been unjustly excluded by a father or brother. Holkar encouraged these applications, and used them to his advantage. The British commander abstained from all interference in such disputes.

punity, the upper provinces of Hindústán, until the establishment of the power of Daulet Rao Sindíá, when the regular brigades, commanded by French officers in the service of that prince, not only checked their inroads, but made all the Sikh chiefs, to the southward of the Satléj, acknowledge obedience and pay tribute to Sindíá: and it was in the contemplation of General Perron, had the war with the English government not occurred, to have subdued the Penjáb, and made the Indus the limit of his possession: and every person acquainted with his means, and with the condition and resources of the Sikhs, must be satisfied he would have accomplished this project with great ease, and at a very early period.

When Holkar fled into the Penjáb, in 1805, and was pursued by that illustrious British commander, Lord Lake, a complete opportunity was given of observing the actual state of this nation, which was found weak and distracted, in a degree that could hardly have been imagined. It was altogether destitute of union. And though a Gúrú-matá, or national council, was called, with a view to decide on those means by which they could best avert the danger by which their country was threatened, from the presence of the English and Mahráta armies, it was attended by few chiefs: and most of the absentees, who had any power, were bold and forward in their offers to resist any resolution to which this council might come. The intrigues and negotiations of all appeared, indeed, at this moment, to be entirely directed to objects of personal resentment, or personal aggrandizement; and every shadow of that concord, which once formed the strength of the Sikh nation, seemed to be extinguished.

SECTION II.

NEITHER the limits of this sketch, nor the materials from which it is drawn, will admit of my giving a particular or correct account of the countries possessed by the Sikhs, or of their forms of government, manners, and habits: but a cursory view of these subjects may be useful, and may excite and direct that curiosity which it cannot expect to gratify.

The country now possessed by the Sikhs, which reaches from latitude 28° 40′ to beyond latitude 32° N., and includes all the Penjáb*, a small part of Multán, and most

* A general estimate of the value of the country possessed by the Sikhs may be formed, when it is stated, that it contains, besides other countries, the whole of the province of Lahore; which, agreeable to Mr. Bernier, produced, in the reign of Aurungzéb, two

of that tract of country which lies between the Jumna and the Satléj, is bounded, to the northward and westward, by the territories of the king of Cábul; to the eastward, by the possessions of the mountaineer Rájás of Jammu, Nadón, and Srínagar; and to the southward, by the territories of the English government, and the sandy deserts of Jasalmér and Hánsyá Hisár.

The Sikhs, who inhabit the country between the Satléj and the Jumna, are called Málawá Singh, and were almost all converted from the Hindú tribes of Játs and Gujars. The title of Málawá Singh was conferred upon them for their extraordinary gallantry, under the Baírágí Banda, who is stated to have declared, that the countries granted to them should be fruitful

hundred and forty-six lacks and ninety-five thousand rupees; or two millions, four hundred and sixty-nine thousand, five hundred pounds sterling.

as Málwá, one of the provinces* in India. The principal chiefs among the Málawá Singhs, are, Sáheb Singh, of Patiálá; B'hangá Singh, of T'hánêsur; B'hág Singh, of Jhind; and B'hailal Singh, of Keintal. Besides these, there are several inferior chiefs, such as Gúrúdah Singh, Jud'h Singh, and Carm Singh; all of whom have a few villages, and some horse, and consider themselves independent; though they, in general, are content to secure their possessions by attaching themselves to one or other of the more powerful leaders.

The country of the Málawá Singh is, in some parts, fruitful: but those districts of it, which border on Hánsyá and Carnál, are very barren; being covered with low wood, and, in many places, almost destitute of water. Sarhind was formerly the capital of

* This province now forms almost the whole territory of Daulet Ráo Sindíá.

this country; but it is now a complete ruin, and has probably never recovered the dreadful ravages of the Bairágí Banda, who is stated not only to have destroyed its mosques, but to have levelled all its palaces and public buildings with the ground. Patiálá is now the largest and most flourishing town of this province, and next to it T'hánésur, which is still held in high religious veneration by the Hindús; who have also a very high reverence for the river Seraswetí, which flows through this province. The territories of the chiefs of Málawá Singh are bounded to the N. W. by the Satléj; between which and the Béyah, is the country called the Jaléndra Beit, or Jaléndra Dúáb; the Sikhs inhabiting which are called the Dúábá Singh, or the Singhs who dwell between the rivers*. The

* With the chiefs of the Sikhs in the Jaléndra Dúáb we are little acquainted. Tárá Singh is the most

country of Jaléndra Dúáb, which reaches from the mountains to the junction of the Satléj and the Béyah, is the most fruitful of all the possessions of the Sikhs; and is, perhaps, excelled in climate and vegetation by no province of India. The soil is light, but very productive: the country, which is open and level, abounds with every kind of grain. That want of water, which is so much felt in other parts of India, must be here unknown; as it is found every where in abundance, within two, or at furthest three, feet from the surface of the soil. The towns of Jaléndra and Sultánpúr are the principal in the Dúáb.

The country between the Béyah and Rávî rivers is called Bári Dúáb, or Mánj'há; and the Sikhs inhabiting it are called

considerable; but he and the others have been greatly weakened by their constant and increasing internal divisions.

Mánj'há Singh. The cities of Lahore and Amritsar are both in this province; and it becomes, in consequence, the great centre of the power of this nation. Ranjit Singh, of Lahore; Fateh Singh*, of Alluwál; and Jud'h Singh, of Rámgadiá†; are the principal chiefs of this country.

The country of Bári is said to be less fertile, particularly towards the mountains, than Jaléndra; but, as it lies on the same level, it must possess nearly the same climate and soil.

The inhabitants of the country between the Rávi and Chanháb, are called D'harpí Singh, from the country being called D'harpí. The D'haníghéb Singh are beyond the Chanháb‡, but within the Jéhalam river.

* Fateh Singh is, like Ranjít Singh, of aJát family.

† Jud'h Singh, of Ramgadiá, is of the carpenter cast.

‡ The term Gujarát Singh is sometimes given to the inhabitants of this Dúáb, of which the chiefs of Gujarát and Rotás are the principal rúlers.

The Sind Singh is the term by which the inhabitants of the districts under the Sikhs, bordering on the Sind, are known; and Nakái Singh is the name given to the Sikhs who reside in Multán. With the leaders of the Sikhs in these provinces, the extent of their possessions, or the climate and productions of the country under their rule, I am little acquainted. Those in Multán, as well as those settled on the river Jéhalam, are said to be constantly engaged in a predatory warfare, either with the officers of the Afghán government, or with Muhammedan chiefs who have jágírs in their vicinity.

The government of the Sikhs, considered in its theory, may, as has been before stated, be termed a theocracy. They obey a temporal chief, it is true; but that chief preserves his power and authority by professing himself the servant of the Khálsá*,

* The word Khálsá, which has before been explained to mean the state or commonwealth, is sup-

or government, which can only be said to act, in times of great public emergency, through the means of a national council, of which every chief is a member, and which is supposed to deliberate and resolve under the immediate inspiration and impulse of an invisible being; who, they believe, always watches over the interests of the commonwealth.

The nature of the power established by the temporal chiefs of the Sikhs, has been sufficiently explained in the narrative of their history. It will be necessary, before any account is given of the forms and actions of their Gúrú-matá, or great national council, which is intended to have a supreme authority over their federative re-

posed, by the Sikhs, to have a mystical meaning, and to imply that superior government, under the protection of which "they live, and to the established rules "and laws of which, as fixed by Gúrú Góvind, it "is their civil and religious duty to conform."

public, to take a view of that body of Acális, or immortals, who, under the double character of fanatic priests and desperate soldiers, have usurped the sole direction of all religious affairs at Amritsar, and are, consequently, leading men in a council which is held at that sacred place, and which deliberates under all the influence of religious enthusiasm.

The Acális* are a class of Sikh devotees; who, agreeably to the historians of that nation, were first founded by Gúrú Góvind, whose institutes, as it has been before stated, they most zealously defended against the innovations of the Bairágí Banda. They wear blue chequered clothes, and bangles,

* Acáli, derived from Acál, a compound term of *cál*, *death*, and the Sanscrit privative *a*, which means *never-dying*, or *immortal*. It is one of the names of the Divinity; and has, probably, been given to this remarkable class of devotees, from their always exclaiming Acál! Acál! in their devotions.

or bracelets of steel*, round their wrists, initiate converts, and have almost the sole direction of the religious ceremonies at Amritsar, where they reside, and of which they deem themselves the defenders; and, consequently, never desire to quit it unless in cases of great extremity.

* All Singhs do not wear bracelets; but it is indispensable to have steel about their persons, which they generally have in the shape of a knife or dagger. In support of this ordinance they quote the following verses of Gúrú Góvind:

> Sáheb beá ki rach'ha hamné,
> Tubi Srí Sáheb, churi, káti, katár—
> Acál purukh ki rach'ha hamné,
> Serv lóh di rach'ha hamné,
> Servacál di rach'ha hamné,
> Serv lohji di sada rach'ha hamné.

which may be translated: "The protection of the "infinite Lord is over us: thou art the lord, the cut-"lass, the knife, and the dagger. The protection of "the immortal Being is over us: the protection of "ALL-STEEL is over us: the protection of ALL-TIME "is over us: the protection of ALL-STEEL is constantly "over us."

This order of Sikhs have a place, or Bungá*, on the bank of the sacred reservoir of Amritsar, where they generally resort, but are individually possessed of property, though they affect poverty, and subsist upon charity; which, however, since their numbers have increased, they generally extort, by accusing the principal chiefs of crimes, imposing fines upon them; and, in the event of their refusing to pay, preventing them from performing their ablutions, or going through any of their religious ceremonies at Amritsar.

It will not, when the above circumstances

* The Shahíd and Nirmala, two other religious tribes among the Sikhs, have Bungás, or places, upon the great reservoir of Amritsar; but both these are peaceful orders of priests, whose duty is to address the Deity, and to read and explain the Adi-Grant'h to the Sikhs. They are, in general, men of some education. A Sikh, of any tribe, may be admitted into either of these classes, as among the Acálís, who admit all into their body who choose to conform to their rules.

are considered, be thought surprising, that the most powerful of the Sikh chiefs should desire to conciliate this body of fanatics, no individual of which can be offended with impunity, as the cause of one is made the cause of the whole; and a chief, who is become unpopular with the Acálís, must not only avoid Amritsar, but is likely to have his dependants taught, when they pay their devotions at that place, that it is pious to resist his authority.

The Acálís have a great interest in maintaining both the religion and government of the Sikhs, as established by Gúrú Góvind; as, on its continuance in that shape, their religious and political influence must depend. Should Amritsar cease to be a place of resort, or be no longer considered as the religious capital of the state, in which all questions that involve the general interests of the commonwealth are to be decided, this formidable order would at once fall from that power and consideration which they now possess, to a level with other mendicants.

When a Gúrú-matá, or great national council, is called, (as it always is, or ought to be, when any imminent danger threatens the country, or any large expedition is to be undertaken,) all the Sikh chiefs assemble at Amritsar. The assembly, which is called the Gúrú-matá, is convened by the Acálís; and when the chiefs meet upon this solemn occasion, it is concluded that all private animosities cease, and that every man sacrifices his personal feelings at the shrine of the general good; and, actuated by principles of pure patriotism, thinks of nothing but the interests of the religion, and commonwealth, to which he belongs.

When the chiefs and principal leaders are seated, the Adi-Grant'h and Dasama Pádsháh ka Grant'h are placed before them. They all bend their heads before these scriptures, and exclaim, *Wá! Gúrújí ka Khálsa! Wá! Gúrújí ki Fateh!* A great quantity of cakes, made of wheat, butter, and sugar, are then placed before the volumes of their sacred writings, and covered with a cloth. These holy cakes, which are in commemoration of the injunction of Nánac, to eat and to give to others to eat, next receive the salutation of the assembly, who then rise, and the Acálís pray aloud, while the musicians play. The Acálís, when the prayers are finished, desire the council to be seated. They sit down, and the cakes being uncovered, are eaten of by all classes* of Sikhs: those distinctions of original tribes, which are, on other occasions, kept up, being on this occasion laid aside, in token of their general and complete union

* A custom of a similar nature, with regard to all tribes eating promiscuously, is observed among the Hindús, at the temple of Jagannáth, where men of all religions and casts, without distinction, eat of the Mahá Prasád, *the great offering;* i. e. food dressed by the cooks of the idols, and sold on the stairs of the temple.

in one cause*. The Acálís then exclaim: "Sirdars! (chiefs) this is a Gúrú-matá!" on which prayers are again said aloud. The chiefs, after this, sit closer, and say to each other: "The sacred Grant'h is betwixt "us, let us swear by our scripture to forget "all internal disputes, and to be united." This moment of religious fervor and ardent patriotism, is taken to reconcile all animosities. They then proceed to consider the danger with which they are threatened, to settle the best plans for averting it, and to choose the generals who are to lead their

* The Sikh priest, who gave an account of this custom, was of a high Hindú tribe; and, retaining some of his prejudices, he at first said, that Muhammedan Sikhs, and those who were converts from the sweeper cast, were obliged, even on this occasion, to eat a little apart from the other Sikhs: but, on being closely questioned, he admitted the fact as stated in the narrative; saying, however, it was only on this solemn occasion that these tribes are admitted to eat with the others.

armies* against the common enemy. The first Gúrú-matá was assembled by Gúrú Góvind; and the latest was called in 1805, when the British army pursued Holkar into the Penjáb.

The principal chiefs of the Sikhs are all descended from Hindú tribes. There is, indeed, no instance of a Singh of a Muhammedan family attaining high power†: a circumstance to be accounted for from the hatred still cherished, by the followers of Gúrú Góvind, against the descendants of

* The army is called, when thus assembled, the Dal Khálsá, or the army of the state.

† The Muhammedans who have become Sikhs, and their descendants, are, in the Penjábi jargon, termed Mezhebi Singh, or Singhs of the faith; and they are subdivided into the four classes which are vulgarly, but erroneously, supposed to distinguish the followers of Muhammed, Sayyad Singh, Sheikh Singh, Moghul Singh, and Patán Singh; by which designations the names of the particular race or country of the Muhammedans have been affixed, by Hindús, as distinctions of cast.

his persecutors: and that this rancorous spirit is undiminished, may be seen from their treatment of the wretched Muhammedans who yet remain in their territories. These, though very numerous, appear to be all poor, and to be an oppressed, despised race. They till the ground, and are employed to carry burdens, and to do all kinds of hard labour: they are not allowed to eat beef, or to say their prayers aloud, and but seldom assemble in their mosques*; of which few, indeed, have escaped destruction. The lower order of Sikhs are more happy: they are protected from the tyranny and violence of the chiefs, under whom they live, by the precepts of their common religion, and by the condition of their country, which enables them to abandon, when-

* The Muhammedan inhabitants of the Penjáb used to flock to the British camp; where, they said, they enjoyed luxuries which no man could appreciate that had not suffered privation. They could pray aloud, and feast upon beef.

ever they choose, a leader whom they dislike; and the distance of a few miles generally places them under the protection of his rival and enemy. It is from this cause that the lowest Sikh horseman usually assumes a very independent style, and the highest chief treats his military followers with attention and conciliation. The civil officers,—to whom the chiefs intrust their accounts, and the management of their property and revenue concerns, as well as the conduct of their negotiations,—are, in general, Sikhs of the Khalása cast; who, being followers of Nánac, and not of Gúrú Góvind, are not devoted to arms, but educated for peaceful occupations, in which they often become very expert and intelligent.

In the collection of the revenue in the Penjáb it is stated to be a general rule, that the chiefs, to whom the territories belong, should receive one half of the produce*, and the farmer the other: but the chief never levies the whole of his share: and in no country, perhaps, is the Rayat, or cultivator, treated with more indulgence. Commerce is not so much encouraged; heavy duties are levied upon it by all petty rulers through whose districts it passes: and this, added to the distracted state in which the Penjáb has been, from the internal disputes of its possessors, caused the rich produce of Cásmír to be carried to India by the difficult and mountainous tract of Jammu, Nadón, and Srínagar. The Sikh chiefs have, however, discovered the injury which their interests have suffered from this cause, and have endeavoured, and not without success, to restore confidence to the merchant; and great part of the shawl trade now flows through the cities of Lahore, Amritsar, and Patiálá, to Hindústán.

* Grain pays in kind; sugar-cane, melons, &c. pay in cash.

The administration of justice in the countries under the Sikhs, is in a very rude and imperfect state; for, though their scriptures inculcate general maxims of justice, they are not considered, as the Old Testament is by the Jews, or the Kóran by the Muhammedans, as books of law: and, having no fixed code, they appear to have adopted that irregular practice, which is most congenial to the temper of the people, and best suited to the unsteady and changing character of their rule of government. The following appears to be the general outline of their practice in the administration of justice.

Trifling disputes about property are settled by the heads of the village, by arbitration*, or by the chiefs. Either of these

* This is called Penchayat, or a court of five; the general number of arbitrators chosen to adjust differences and disputes. It is usual to assemble a Pan chayat, or a court of arbitration, in every part of India, under a native government; and, as they are always

modes, supposing the parties consent to refer to it, is final; and they must agree to one or other. If a theft occurs, the property is recovered, and the party punished by the person from whom it was stolen, who is aided on such occasions by the inhabitants of his village, or his chief. The punishment, however, is never capital*. Murder is generally revenged by the relations of the deceased, who, in such cases, rigorously retaliate on the murderer, and often on all who endeavour to protect him.

chosen from men of the best reputation in the place where they meet, this court has a high character for justice.

* A Sikh priest, who has been several years in Calcutta, gave this outline of the administration of justice among his countrymen. He spoke of it with rapture; and insisted, with true patriotic prejudice, on its great superiority over the vexatious system of the English government; which was, he said, tedious, vexatious, and expensive, and advantageous only to clever rogues.

The character of the Sikhs, or rather Singhs, which is the name by which the followers of Gúrú Góvind, who are all devoted to arms, are distinguished, is very marked. They have, in general, the Hindú cast of countenance, somewhat altered by their long beards, and are to the full as active as the Mahrátas; and much more robust, from their living fuller, and enjoying a better and colder climate. Their courage is equal, at all times, to that of any natives of India; and when wrought upon by prejudice or religion, is quite desperate. They are all horsemen, and have no infantry in their own country, except for the defence of their forts and villages, though they generally serve as infantry in foreign armies. They are bold, and rather rough, in their address; which appears more to a stranger from their invariably speaking in a loud tone*

* Talking aloud is so habitual to a Sikh, that he bawls a secret in your ear. It has often occurred to me, that they have acquired it from living in a country

of voice: but this is quite a habit, and is alike used by them to express the sentiments of regard and hatred. The Sikhs have been reputed deceitful and cruel; but I know no grounds upon which they can be considered more so than the other tribes of India. They seemed to me, from all the intercourse I had with them, to be more open and sincere than the Mahrátas, and less rude and savage than the Afghâns. They have, indeed, become, from national success, too proud of their own strength, and too irritable in their tempers, to have patience for the wiles of the former; and they retain, in spite of their change of manners and religion, too much of the original

where internal disputes have so completely destroyed confidence, that they can only carry on conversation with each other at a distance: but it is fairer, perhaps, to impute this boisterous and rude habit to their living almost constantly in a camp, in which the voice certainly loses that nice modulated tone which distinguishes the more polished inhabitants of cities.

character of their Hindú ancestors, (for the great majority are of the Hindú race,) to have the constitutional ferocity of the latter. The Sikh soldier is, generally speaking, brave, active, and cheerful, without polish, but neither destitute of sincerity nor attachment; and if he often appears wanting in humanity, it is not so much to be attributed to his national character, as to the habits of a life, which, from the condition of the society in which he is born, is generally passed in scenes of violence and rapine.

The Sikh merchant, or cultivator of the soil, if he is a Singh, differs little in character from the soldier, except that his occupation renders him less presuming and boisterous. He also wears arms, and is, from education, prompt to use them whenever his individual interest, or that of the community in which he lives*, requires him

* The old Sikh soldier generally returns to his native village, where his wealth, courage, or experience, always obtains him respect, and sometimes station and

to do so. The general occupations of the Khalása Sikhs has been before mentioned.

consequence. The second march which the British army made into the country of the Sikhs, the head-quarters were near a small village, the chief of which, who was upwards of a hundred years of age, had been a soldier, and retained all the look and manner of his former occupation. He came to me, and expressed his anxiety to see Lord Lake. I showed him the general, who was sitting alone, in his tent, writing. He smiled, and said he knew better: "The hero who had "overthrown Sindiá and Holkár, and had conquered "Hindústan, must be surrounded with attendants, and "have plenty of persons to write for him." I assured him that it was Lord Lake; and, on his lordship coming to breakfast, I introduced the old Singh, who seeing a number of officers collect round him, was at last satisfied of the truth of what I said; and, pleased with the great kindness and condescension with which he was treated by one whom he justly thought so great a man, sat down on the carpet, became quite talkative, and related all he had seen, from the invasion of Nádir Shah to that moment. Lord Lake, pleased with the bold manliness of his address, and the independence of his sentiments, told him he would grant him any favour he wished. "I am glad of it,"

Their character differs widely from that of the Singhs. Full of intrigue, pliant, versatile, and insinuating, they have all the art of the lower classes of Hindús, who are usually employed in transacting business: from whom, indeed, as they have no distinction of dress, it is very difficult to distinguish them.

The religious tribes of Acális, Shahíd, and Nirmala, have been noticed. Their

said the old man; "then march away with your army "from my village, which will otherwise be destroyed." Lord Lake, struck with the noble spirit of the request, assured him he would march next morning, and that, in the mean-time, he should have guards, who would protect his village from injury. Satisfied with this assurance, the old Singh was retiring, apparently full of admiration and gratitude at Lord Lake's goodness, and of wonder at the scene he had witnessed, when, meeting two officers at the door of the tent, he put a hand upon the breast of each, exclaiming at the same time, "*Brothers! where were you born, and where are* "*you at this moment?*" and, without waiting for an answer, proceeded to his village.

general character is formed from their habits of life. The Acális are insolent, ignorant, and daring: presuming upon those rights which their numbers and fanatic courage have established, their deportment is hardly tolerant to the other Sikhs, and insufferable to strangers, for whom they entertain a contempt, which they take little pains to conceal. The Shahíd and the Nirmala, particularly the latter, have more knowledge, and more urbanity. They are almost all men of quiet, peaceable habits; and many of them are said to possess learning.

There is another tribe among the Sikhs, called the Nánac Pautra, or descendants of Nánac, who have the character of being a mild, inoffensive race; and, though they do not acknowledge the institutions of Gúrú Góvind, they are greatly revered by his followers, who hold it sacrilege to injure the race of their founder; and, under the advantage which this general veneration affords them, the Nánac Pautra pursue their occupations; which, if they are not mendicants, is generally that of travelling merchants. They do not carry arms; and profess, agreeably to the doctrine of Nánac, to be at peace* with all mankind.

The Sikh converts, it has been before stated, continue, after they have quitted their original religion, all those civil usages and customs of the tribes to which they belonged, that they can practise, without infringing the tenets of Nánac, or the institutions of Gúrú Góvind. They are most particular with regard to their intermarriages; and, on this point, Sikhs descended from Hindús almost invariably conform to Hindú customs, every tribe intermarrying within

* When Lord Lake entered the Penjáb, in 1805, a general protection was requested, by several principal chiefs, for the Nánac Pautra, on the ground of the veneration in which they were held, which enabled them, it was stated, to travel all over the country without molestation, even when the most violent wars existed. It was, of course, granted.

itself. The Hindú usage, regarding diet, is also held equally sacred; no Sikh, descended from a Hindú family, ever violating it, except upon particular occasions, such as a Gúrú-matá, when they are obliged, by their tenets and institutions, to eat promiscuously. The strict observance of these usages has enabled many of the Sikhs, particularly of the Ját* and Gujar† tribes, which include almost all those settled to the south of the Satléj, to preserve an intimate intercourse with their original tribes; who, considering the Sikhs not as having lost cast, but as Hindús that have joined a political associa-

* The Játs are Hindús of a low tribe, who, taking advantage of the decline of the Moghul empire, have, by their courage and enterprise, raised themselves into some consequence on the north-western parts of Hindustan, and many of the strongest forts of that part of India are still in their possession.

† The Gujars, who are also Hindús, have raised themselves to power by means not dissimilar to those used by the Játs. Almost all the thieves in Hindústan are of this tribe.

tion, which obliges them to conform to general rules established for its preservation, neither refuse to intermarry* nor to eat with them.

The higher cast of Hindús, such as Brahmens and Cshatriyas, who have become Sikhs, continue to intermarry with converts of their own tribes, but not with Hindús of the cast they have abandoned, as they are polluted by eating animal food; all kinds of which are lawful to Sikhs, except the cow, which it is held sacrilege to slay†. Nánac, whose object was to conciliate the Muhammedans to his creed, prohibited hog's flesh also; but it was introduced by his successors, as much, perhaps, from a spirit of revenge against the Moslems, as from considerations of indulgence to the

* A marriage took place very lately between the Sikh chief of Patiálá, and that of the Ját Rájá, of B'haratpúr.

† Their prejudice regarding the killing of cows is stronger, if possible, than that of the Hindús.

numerous converts of the Ját and Gujar tribe, among whom wild hog is a favourite species of food.

The Muhammedans, who become Sikhs, intermarry with each other, but are allowed to preserve none of their usages, being obliged to eat hog's flesh, and abstain from circumcision.

The Sikhs are forbid the use of tobacco*, but allowed to indulge in spirituous† liquors, which they almost all drink to excess; and it is rare to see a Singh soldier, after sunset, quite sober. Their drink is an

* The Khalása Sikhs, who follow Nánac, and reject Gúrú Góvind's institutions, make use of it.

† Spirituous liquors, they say, are allowed by that verse in the Adi-Grant'h, which states, "Eat, and give "unto others to eat. Drink, and give unto others to "drink. Be glad, and make others glad." There is also an authority, quoted by the Sikhs, from the Hindú Sástras, in favour of this drinking to excess. Durgá, agreeably to the Sikh quotations, used to drink, because liquor inspires courage; and this goddess, they say, was drunk when she slew Mahíshásur.

ardent spirit*, made in the Penjáb; but they have no objections to either the wine or spirits of Europe, when they can obtain them.

The use of opium, to intoxicate, is very common with the Sikhs, as with most of the military tribes of India. They also take B'hang†, another inebriating drug.

The conduct of the Sikhs to their women differs in no material respect from that of the tribes of Hindús, or Muhammedans, from whom they are descended. Their moral character with regard to women, and

* When Fateh Singh, of Aluwál, who was quite a young man, was with the British army, Lord Lake gratified him by a field review. He was upon an elephant, and I attended him upon another. A little before sunset he became low and uneasy. I observed it; and B'hág Singh, an old chief, of frank, rough manners, at once said, "Fateh Singh wants his dram, but "is ashamed to drink before you." I requested he would follow his custom, which he did, by drinking a large cup of spirits.

† Cannabis sativa.

indeed in most other points, may, from the freedom of their habits, generally be considered as much more lax than that of their ancestors, who lived under the restraint of severe restrictions, and whose fear of excommunication from their cast, at least obliged them to cover their sins with the veil of decency. This the emancipated Sikhs despise: and there is hardly an infamy which this debauched and dissolute race are not accused (and I believe with justice) of committing in the most open and shameful manner.

The Sikhs are almost all horsemen, and they take great delight in riding. Their horses were, a few years ago, famous; and those bred in the Lak'hi Jungle, and other parts of their territory, were justly celebrated for their strength, temper, and activity: but the internal distractions of these territories has been unfavourable to the encouragement of the breed, which has consequently declined; and the Sikhs now are in no respect better mounted than the Mahrátas. From a hundred of their cavalry it would be difficult to select ten horses that would be admitted as fit to mount native troopers in the English service.

Their horsemen use swords and spears, and most of them now carry matchlocks, though some still use the bow and arrow; a species of arms, for excellence in the use of which their forefathers were celebrated, and which their descendants appear to abandon with great reluctance.

The education of the Sikhs renders them hardy, and capable of great fatigue; and the condition of the society in which they live, affords constant exercise to that restless spirit of activity and enterprise which their religion has generated. Such a race cannot be epicures: they appear, indeed, generally to despise luxury of diet, and pride themselves in their coarse fare. Their dress is also plain, not unlike that of the Hindús, equally light and divested of ornament. Some of the chiefs wear gold bangles; but this is rare; and the general characteristic of their dress and mode of living, is simplicity.

The principal leaders among the Sikhs affect to be familiar and easy of intercourse with their inferiors, and to despise the pomp and state of the Muhammedan chiefs: but their pride often counteracts this disposition; and they appeared to me to have, in proportion to their rank and consequence, more state, and to maintain equal, if not more, reserve and dignity with their followers, than is usual with the Mahráta chiefs.

It would be difficult, if not impracticable, to ascertain the amount of the population of the Sikh territories, or even to compute the number of the armies which they could bring into action. They boast that they can raise more than a hundred thousand horse: and, if it were possible to assemble every Sikh horseman, this statement might not be an exaggeration: but there is, perhaps, no chief among them, except Ranjit Singh, of Lahore, that could bring an effective body of four thousand men into the field. The force of Ranjit Singh did not, in 1805, amount to eight thousand; and part of that was under chiefs who had been subdued from a state of independence, and whose turbulent minds ill brooked an usurpation which they deemed subversive of the constitution of their commonwealth. His army is now more numerous than it was, but it is composed of materials which have no natural cohesion; and the first serious check which it meets, will probably cause its dissolution.

SECTION III.

THERE is no branch of this sketch which is more curious and important, or that offers more difficulties to the inquirer, than the religion of the Sikhs. We meet with a creed of pure deism, grounded on the most sublime general truths, blended with the belief of all the absurdities of the Hindú mythology, and the fables of Muhammedanism; for Nánac professed a desire to reform, not to destroy, the religion of the tribe in which he was born; and, actuated by the great and benevolent design of reconciling the jarring faiths of Brahmá and Muhammed, he endeavoured to conciliate both Hindús and Moslems to his doctrine, by persuading them to reject those parts of their respective beliefs and usages, which, he contended, were unworthy of that God whom they both adored. He called upon the Hindús to abandon the worship of idols, and to return to that pure devotion of the Deity, in which their religion originated. He called upon the Muhammedans to abstain from practices, like the slaughter of cows, that were offensive to the religion of the Hindús, and to cease from the persecution of that race. He adopted, in order to conciliate them, many of the maxims which he had learnt from mendicants, who professed the principles of the Súfi sect; and he constantly referred to the admired writings of the celebrated Muhammedan Kabír*, who was a professed Súfi, and who

* This celebrated Súfi, or philosophical deist, lived in the time of the Emperor Shér Sháh. He was, by trade, a weaver; but has written several admired works. They are all composed in a strain of universal philanthropy and benevolence; and, above all, he inculcated religious toleration, particularly between the Muhammedans and Hindús, by both of whom his memory is held in the highest esteem and veneration.

inculcated the doctrine of the equality of the relation of all created beings to their Creator. Nánac endeavoured, with all the power of his own genius, aided by such authorities, to impress both Hindús and Muhammedans with a love of toleration and an abhorrence of war; and his life was as peaceable as his doctrine. He appears, indeed, to have adopted, from the hour in which he abandoned his worldly occupations to that of his death, the habits practised by that crowd of holy mendicants, Sanyásís and Fakírs, with whom India swarms. He conformed to their customs; and his extraordinary austerities* are a constant theme of praise with his followers. His works are all in praise of God; but he

* Nánac was celebrated for the manner in which he performed Tapasa, or austere devotion, which requires the mind to be so totally absorbed in the Divinity, as to be abstracted from every worldly thought, and this for as long a period as human strength is capable of sustaining.

treats the polytheism of the Hindús with respect, and even veneration. He never shows a disposition to destroy the fabric, but only wishes to divest it of its useless tinsel and false ornaments, and to establish its complete dependence upon the great Creator of the universe. He speaks every where of Muhammed, and his successors, with moderation; but animadverts boldly on what he conceives to be their errors; and, above all, on their endeavours to propagate their faith by the sword.

As Nánac made no material invasion of either the civil or religious usages of the Hindús, and as his only desire was to restore a nation who had degenerated from their original pure worship* into idolatry, he may be considered more in the light of a reformer than of a subverter of the Hindú

* The most ancient Hindús do not appear to have paid adoration to idols; but, though they adored God, they worshipped the sun and elements.

religion; and those Sikhs who adhere to his tenets, without admitting those of Gúrú Góvind, are hardly to be distinguished from the great mass of Hindú population; among whom there are many sects who differ, much more than that of Nánac, from the general and orthodox worship at present established in India.

The first successors of Nánac appear to have taught exactly the same doctrine as their leader; and though Har Góvind armed all his followers, it was on a principle of self-defence, in which he was fully justified, even by the usage of the Hindús. It was reserved for Gúrú Góvind to give a new character to the religion of his followers; not by making any material alteration in the tenets of Nánac, but by establishing institutions and usages, which not only separated them from other Hindús, but which, by the complete abolition of all distinction of casts, destroyed, at one blow, a system of civil polity, that, from being interwoven with the religion of a weak and bigoted race, fixed the rule of its priests upon a basis that had withstood the shock of ages. Though the code of the Hindús was calculated to preserve a vast community in tranquillity and obedience to its rulers, it had the natural effect of making the country, in which it was established, an easy conquest to every powerful foreign invader; and it appears to have been the contemplation of this effect that made Gúrú Góvind resolve on the abolition of cast, as a necessary and indispensable prelude to any attempt to arm the original native population of India against their foreign tyrants. He called upon all Hindús to break those chains in which prejudice and bigotry had bound them, and to devote themselves to arms, as the only means by which they could free themselves from the oppressive government of the Muhammedans; against whom, a sense of his own wrongs, and those of his tribe, led him to preach eternal warfare. His religious doctrine was meant to be popular, and it promised equality. The invidious appellations of Bráhmen, Cshatriya, Vaisya, and Súdra, were abolished. The pride of descent might remain, and keep up some distinctions; but, in the religious code of Góvind, every Khálsa Singh (for such he termed his followers) was equal, and had a like title to the good things of this world, and to the blessings of a future life.

Though Gúrú Góvind mixes, even more than Nánac, the mythology of the Hindús with his own tenets; though his desire to conciliate them, in opposition to the Muhammedans, against whom he always breathed war and destruction, led him to worship at Hindú sacred shrines; and though the peculiar customs and dress among his followers, are stated to have been adopted from veneration to the Hindú goddess of courage, Dúrga Bhaváni; yet it is impossible to reconcile the religion and usages, which Góvind has established, with the belief of the Hindús. It does not, like that of Nánac, question some favourite dogmas of the disciples of Brahmá, and attack that worship of idols, which few of these defend, except upon the ground of these figures, before which they bend, being symbolical representations of the attributes of an all-powerful Divinity; but it proceeds at once to subvert the foundation of the whole system. Wherever the religion of Gúrú Góvind prevails, the institutions of Brahmá must fall. The admission of proselytes, the abolition of the distinctions of cast, the eating of all kinds of flesh, except that of cows, the form of religious worship, and the general devotion of all Singhs to arms, are ordinances altogether irreconcileable with Hindú mythology, and have rendered the religion of the Sikhs as obnoxious to the Bráhmens, and higher tribes of the Hindús, as it is popular with the lower orders of that numerous class of mankind.

After this rapid sketch of the general character of the religion of the Sikhs, I shall take a more detailed view of its origin, progress, tenets, and forms.

A Sikh author*, whom I have followed in several parts of this sketch, is very particular in stating the causes of the origin of the religion of Nánac: he describes the different Yugas, or ages of the world, stated in the Hindú mythology. The Cali Yug, which is the present, is that in which it was written that the human race would become completely depraved: "Discord," says the author, speaking of the Cali Yug, "will "rise in the world, sin prevail, and the "universe become wicked; cast will con- "tend with cast; and, like bamboos in "friction, consume each other to embers. "The Védas, or scriptures," he adds, "will "be held in disrepute, for they shall not "be understood, and the darkness of igno-

* B'hai Gúrú Dás B'halé.

" rance will prevail every where." Such is this author's record of a divine prophecy regarding this degenerate age. He proceeds to state what has ensued: " Every one fol-" lowed his own path, and sects were " separated; some worshipped Chandra " (the moon); some Surya (the sun); some " prayed to the earth, to the sky, and the " air, and the water, and the fire, while " others worshipped D'herma Rájá (the " judge of the dead); and in the fallacy of " the sects nothing was to be found but " error. In short, pride prevailed in the " world, and the four casts* established a " system of ascetic devotion. From these, " the ten sects of Sanyásís, and the twelve " sects of Yógis, originated. The Jangam, " the Srívíra, and the Déva Digambar, " entered into mutual contests. The Bráh-" mens divided into different classes; and

* Bráhmen, Cshatriya, Vaisya, and Súdra.

"the Sastras, Védas, and Puránas*, contradicted each other. The six Dersans (philosophical sects) exhibited enmity, and the thirty-six Páshands (heterodox sects) arose, with hundreds of thousands of chimerical and magical (*tantra mantra*) sects: and thus, from one form, many good and many evil forms originated, and error prevailed in the Cali Yug, or age of general depravity."

The Sikh author pursues this account of the errors into which the Hindús fell, with a curious passage regarding the origin and progress of the Muhammedan religion.

"The world," he writes, "went on with these numerous divisions, when Muhammed Yara† appeared, who gave origin

* Different sacred books of the Hindús.

† Yár signifies *friend*; and one of the prophet's titles, among his followers, is Yar-i-Khudá, or *the Friend of God*.

" to the seventy-two sects*, and widely " disseminated discord and war. He esta-" blished the Rózeh o Aíd (fast and festi-" vals), and the Namáz (prayer), and " made his practice of devotional acts pre-" valent in the world, with a multitude of " distinctions, of Pír (saint), Paighamber " (prophet), Ulemá (the order of priest-" hood), and Kitàb (the Koran). He de-" molished the temples, and on their ruins " built the mosques, slaughtering cows " and helpless persons, and spreading trans-" gression far and wide, holding in hostility " Cáfirs (infidels), Mulhids (idolaters), Ir-" menis (Armenians), Rumis (the Turks), " and Zingis (Ethiopians). Thus vice " greatly diffused itself in the universe."

" Then," this author adds, " there were " two races in the world; the one Hindú, " the other Muhammedan; and both were

* The Muhammedan religion is said to be divided into seventy-two sects.

" alike excited by pride, enmity, and ava-
" rice, to violence. The Hindús set their
" heart on Gangá and Benares; the Mu-
" hammedans on Mecca and the Cáaba:
" the Hindús clung to their mark on the
" forehead and brahminical string; the
" Moslemans to their circumcision: the
" one cried Rám (the name of an Avatár),
" the other Rahím (the merciful); one
" name, but two ways of pronouncing it;
" forgetting equally the Védas and the
" Koràn: and through the deceptions of
" lust, avarice, the world, and Satan, they
" swerved equally from the true path:
" while Bráhmens and Moulavis destroyed
" each other by their quarrels, and the
" vicissitudes of life and death hung always
" suspended over their heads.

" When the world was in this distracted
" state, and vice prevailed," says this writer,
" the complaint of virtue, whose dominion
" was extinct, reached the throne of the
" Almighty, who created Nánac, to en-

"lighten and improve a degenerate and "corrupt age: and that holy man made "God the Supreme known to all, giving "the nectareous water that washed his feet "to his disciples to drink. He restored to "Virtue her strength, blended the four "casts* into one, established one mode of "salutation, changed the childish play of "bending the head at the feet of idols, "taught the worship of the true God, and "reformed a depraved world."

Nánac appears, by the account of this author, to have established his fame for sanctity by the usual modes of religious mendicants. He performed severe Tapasa†, living upon sand and swallow-wort, and sleeping on sharp pebbles; and, after attain-

* There is no ground to conclude that casts were altogether abolished by Nánac; though his doctrines and writings had a tendency to equalize the Hindús, and unite all in the worship of one God.

† A kind of ascetic devotion, which has been before explained.

ing fame by this kind of penance, he commenced his travels, with the view of spreading his doctrine over the earth.

After Nánac had completed his terrestrial travels, he is supposed to have ascended to Suméru, where he saw the Sidd'his*, all seated in a circle. These, from a knowledge of that eminence for which he was predestined, wished to make him assume the characteristic devotion of their sect, to which they thought he would be an ornament. While means were used to effect this purpose, a divine voice was heard to exclaim: "Nánac shall form his "own sect, distinct from all the Yatís† "and Sidd'his; and his name shall be "joyful to the Cali Yug." After this,

* The Sidd'his (saints) are the attendants of the gods. The name is most generally applied to those who wait on Ganésa.

† The name Yatí is most usually applied to the priests of the Jainas; but it is also applicable to Sanyásís, and other penitents.

Nánac preached the adoration of the true God to the Hindús; and then went to instruct the Muhammedans, in their sacred temples at Mecca. When at that place, the holy men are said to have gathered round him, and demanded, Whether their faith, or that of the Hindús, was the best? "Without the practice of true piety, both," said Nánac, "are erroneous, and neither "Hindús nor Moslems will be acceptable "before the throne of God; for the faded "tinge of scarlet, that has been soiled by "water, will never return. You both de-"ceive yourselves, pronouncing aloud Rám "and Rahím, and the way of Satan pre-"vails in the universe."

The courageous independence with which Nánac announced his religion to the Muhammedans, is a favourite topic with his biographers. He was one day abused, and even struck, as one of these relates, by a Moullah, for lying on the ground with his feet in the direction of the sacred temple of

Mecca. "How darest thou, infidel!" said the offended Muhammedan priest, "turn "thy feet towards the house of God!"— "Turn them, if you can," said the pious but indignant Nánac, "in a direction where "the house of God is not."

Nánac did not deny the mission of Muhammed. "That prophet was sent," he said, "by God, to this world, to do good, "and to disseminate the knowledge of one "God through means of the Kóran; but "he, acting on the principle of free-will, "which all human beings exercise, intro-"duced oppression, and cruelty, and the "slaughter of cows*, for which he died.— "I am now sent," he added, "from heaven, "to publish unto mankind a book, which "shall reduce all the names given unto "God to one name, which is God; and he "who calls him by any other, shall fall into

* Nánac appears on this, and every other occasion, to have preserved his attachment to this favourite dogma of the Hindús.

"the path of the devil, and have his feet "bound in the chains of wretchedness. "You have," said he to the Muhammedans, "despoiled the temples, and burnt "the sacred Védas, of the Hindús; and "you have dressed yourselves in dresses of "blue, and you delight to have your "praises sung from house to house: but I, "who have seen all the world, tell you, "that the Hindús equally hate you and "your mosques. I am sent to reconcile "your jarring faiths, and I implore you to "read their scriptures, as well as your own: "but reading is useless without obedience "to the doctrine taught; for God has "said, no man shall be saved except he "has performed good works. The Almighty will not ask to what tribe or "persuasion he belongs. He will only "ask, What has he done? Therefore those "violent and continued disputes, which "subsist between the Hindús and Moslemans, are as impious as they are unjust."

Such were the doctrines, according to his disciples, which Nánac taught to both Hindús and Muhammedans. He professed veneration and respect, but refused adoration to the founders of both their religions; for which, as for those of all other tribes, he had great tolerance. "A hundred thousand "of Muhammeds," said Nánac, "a million "of Brahmás, Vishnus, and a hundred "thousand Rámas, stand at the gate of the "Most High. These all perish; God alone "is immortal. Yet men, who unite in "the praise of God, are not ashamed "of living in contention with each other; "which proves that the evil spirit has "subdued all. He alone is a true Hindû "whose heart is just; and he only is "a good Muhammedan whose life is "pure."

Nánac is stated, by the Sikh author from whom the above account of his religion is taken, to have had an interview with the supreme God, which he thus describes:

" One day Nánac heard a voice from " above exclaim, Nánac, approach!" He replied, " Oh God! what power have I to " stand in thy presence?" The voice said, " Close thine eyes." Nánac shut his eyes, and advanced: he was told to look up: he did so, and heard the word *Wa!* or *well done*, pronounced five times; and then *Wa! Gúrújí*, or *well done teacher*. After this God said, " Nánac! I have sent thee into " the world, in the Cáli Yug (or depraved " age); go and bear my name." Nánac said, " Oh God! how can I bear the mighty " burthen? If my age was extended to " tens of millions of years, if I drank of " immortality, and my eyes were formed of " the sun and moon, and were never closed, " still, oh God! I could not presume to " take charge of thy wondrous name."— " I will be thy Gúrú (teacher)," said God, " and thou shalt be a Gúrú to all mankind, " and thy sect shall be great in the world; " their word is Púrí Púrí. The word

" of the Bairágí is Ram! Rám! that of the " Sanyásí, Om! Namá! Náráyen! and the " word of the Yógís, Adés! Adés! and the " salutation of the Muhammedans is Salám " Alíkam; and that of the Hindús, Rám! " Ram! but the word of thy sect shall be " Gúrú, and I will forgive the crimes of " thy disciples. The place of worship of " the Bairágís is called Rámsála; that of " the Yógís, Asan; that of the Sanyásís, " Mát; that of thy tribe shall be Dherma " Sála. Thou must teach unto thy fol- " lowers three lessons: the first, to worship " my name; the second, charity; the third, " ablution. They must not abandon the " world, and they must do ill to no being; " for into every being have I infused breath; " and whatever I am, thou art, for betwixt " us there is no difference. It is a blessing " that thou art sent into the Cáli Yug." After this, " *Wa Gúrú!* or *well done,* " *teacher!* was pronounced from the mouth " of the most high Gúrú or teacher (God),

" and Nánac came to give light and free-
" dom to the universe."

The above will give a sufficient view of the ideas which the Sikhs entertain regarding the divine origin of their faith; which, as first taught by Nánac, might justly be deemed the religion of peace.

" Put on armour," says Nánac, " that " will harm no one; let thy coat of mail " be that of understanding, and convert " thy enemies to friends. Fight with va- " lour, but with no weapon except the " word of God." All the principles which Nánac inculcated, were those of pure deism; but moderated, in order to meet the deep-rooted usages of that portion of mankind which he wished to reclaim from error. Though he condemned the lives and habits of the Muhammedans, he approved of the Korán*. He admitted the truth of the

* This fact is admitted by Sikh authors. It is, however, probable, that Nánac was but imperfectly acquainted with the doctrines of that volume.

ancient Védas, but contended that the Hindú religion had been corrupted, by the introduction of a plurality of gods, with the worship of images; which led their minds astray from that great and eternal Being, to whom adoration should alone be paid. He, however, followed the forms of the Hindús, and adopted most of their doctrines which did not interfere with his great and leading tenet. He admitted the claim to veneration, of the numerous catalogue of Hindú Dévas, and Dévatás, or inferior deities; but he refused them adoration. He held it impious to slaughter the cow; and he directed his votaries, as has been seen, to consider ablution as one of their primary religious duties.

Nánac, according to Penjábi authors, admitted the Hindú doctrine of metempsychosis. He believed, that really good men would enjoy Paradise; that those, who had no claim to the name of good, but yet were not bad, would undergo another probation, by revisiting the world in the human form: and that the bad would animate the bodies of animals, particularly dogs and cats: but it appears, from the same authorities, that Nánac was acquainted with the Muhammedan doctrine regarding the fall of man, and a future state; and that he represented it to his followers as a system, in which God, by showing a heaven and a hell, had, in his great goodness, held out future rewards and punishments to man, whose will he had left free, to incite him to good actions, and deter him from bad. The principle of reward and punishment is so nearly the same in the Hindú and in the Muhammedan religion, that it was not difficult for Nánac to reconcile his followers upon this point: but in this, as in all others, he seems to have bent to the doctrine of Brahma. In all his writings, however, he borrowed indifferently from the Korán and the Hindú Sástras; and his example was followed by his successors; and quotations from the scriptures of the Hindús, and from the book of Muhammed, are indiscriminately introduced into all their sacred writings, to elucidate those points on which it was their object to reconcile these jarring religions.

With the exact mode in which Nánac instructed his followers to address their prayers to that supreme Being whom he taught them to adore, I am not acquainted. Their D'herma Sála, or temples of worship, are, in general, plain buildings. Images are, of course, banished. Their prescribed forms of prayer are, I believe, few and simple. Part of the writings of Nánac, which have since been incorporated with those of his successors, in the Adi Grant'h, are read, or rather recited, upon every solemn occasion. These are all in praise of the Deity, of religion, and of virtue; and against impiety and immorality. The Adi Grant'h, the whole of the first part of which is ascribed to Nánac, is written, like the rest of the books of the Sikhs, in the

Gúrúmuk'h* character. I can only judge very imperfectly of the value of this work: but some extracts, translated from it, appear worthy of that admiration which is bestowed upon it by the Sikhs.

The Adi-Grant'h is in verse; and many of the chapters, written by Nánac, are termed Pídi, which means, literally, a ladder or flight of steps; and, metaphorically, that by which a man ascends.

In the following fragment, literally translated from the Sódar rág ásá mahilla pehla of Nánac, he displays the supremacy of the true God, and the inferiority of the Dévatás, and other created beings, to the universal Creator; however they may have been elevated into deities by ignorance or superstition.

> Thy portals, how wonderful they are, how wonderful thy palace, where thou sittest and governest all!
> Numberless and infinite are the sounds which proclaim thy praises.

* A modified species of the Nágari character.

How numerous are thy Peris, skilful in music and song!

Pavan (air), water, and Vasantar (fire), celebrate thee; D'herma Rájá (the Hindú Rhadamanthus) celebrates thy praises, at thy gates.

Chitragupta (Secretary to D'herma Rájá) celebrates thy praises; who, skilful in writing, writes and administers final justice.

Iswara, Brahma, and Dévi, celebrate thy praises; they declare in fit terms thy majesty, at thy gates.

Indra celebrates thy praises, sitting on the Indraic throne amid the Dévatás.

The just celebrate thy praises in profound meditation, the pious declare thy glory.

The Yatís and the Satís joyfully celebrate thy might.

The Pandits, skilled in reading, and the Rishíswaras, who, age by age, read the Védas, recite thy praises.

The Móhinís (celestial courtezans), heart alluring, inhabiting Swarga, Mritya, and Pátálá, celebrate thy praises.

The Ratnas (gems), with the thirty-eight Tírt'has (sacred springs), celebrate thy praises.

Heroes of great might celebrate thy name; beings of the four kinds of production celebrate thy praises.

The continents, and regions of the world, celebrate thy praises; the universal Brahmánda (the mundane egg), which thou hast established firm.

All who know thee praise thee, all who are desirous of thy worship.

How numerous they are who praise thee! they exceed my comprehension: how, then, shall Nánac describe them?

He, even he, is the Lord of truth, true, and truly just.

He is, he was, he passes, he passes not, the preserver of all that is preserved.

Of numerous hues, sorts and kinds, he is the original author of Máyá (deception).

Having formed the creation, he surveys his own work, the display of his own greatness.

What pleases him he does, and no order of any other being can reach him.

He is the Pádsháh and the Pádsáheb of Sháhs; Nánac resides in his favour.

These few verses are, perhaps, sufficient to show, that it was on a principle of pure deism that Nánac entirely grounded his religion. It was not possible, however, that the minds of any large portion of mankind could remain long fixed in a belief which presented them only with general truths, and those of a nature too vast for their contemplation or comprehension. The followers of Nánac, since his death, have paid an adoration to his name, which is at variance with the lessons which he taught; they have clothed him in all the attributes of a saint: they consider him as the selected instrument of God to make known the true faith to fallen man; and, as such, they give him divine honours; not only performing pilgrimage to his tomb, but addressing him, in their prayers, as their saviour and mediator.

The religious tenets and usages of the Sikhs continued, as they had been established by Nánac*, till the time of Gúrú

* Certainly no material alteration was made, either in the belief or forms of the Sikhs, by any of his successors before Gúrú Góvind. Har Góvind, who armed his followers to repel aggression, would only appear to have made a temporary effort to oppose his

Góvind; who, though he did not alter the fundamental principles of the established faith, made so complete a change in the sacred usages and civil habits of his followers, that he gave them an entirely new character: and though the Sikhs retain all their veneration for Nánac, they deem Gúrú Góvind to have been equally exalted, by the immediate favour and protection of the Divinity; and the Dásama Pádsháh ka Gran'th, or book of the tenth king, which was written by Gúrú Góvind, is considered, in every respect, as holy as the Adí Grant'h of Nánac, and his immediate successors. I cannot better explain the pretensions which Gúrú Góvind has made to the rank of a prophet, than by exhibiting his own account of his mission in a literal version from his Vichitra Nátac.

enemies, without an endeavour to effect any serious change in the religious belief or customs of the sect to which he belonged.

"I now declare my own history, and "the multifarious austerities which I have "performed.

"Where the seven peaks rise beautiful "on the mountain Hémacuta, and the "place takes the name of Sapta Sringa, "greater penance have I performed than "was ever endured by Pándu Rájá, medi-"tating constantly on Mahá Cál and Cálica, "till diversity was changed into one form. "My father and mother meditated on the "Divinity, and performed the Yóga, till "Gúrú Déva approved of their devotions. "Then the Supreme issued his order, and "I was born, in the Calí Yug, though my "inclination was not to come into the "world, my mind being fixed on the foot "of the Supreme. When the supreme "Being made known his will, I was sent "into the world. The eternal Being thus "addressed this feeble insect:

"—I have manifested thee as my own "son, and appointed thee to establish a

"perfect Pant'h (sect). Go into the world,
"establish virtue and expel vice."—

"—I stand with joined hands, bending "my head at thy word: the Pant'h shall "prevail in the world, when thou lendest "thine aid.—Then was I sent into the "world: thus I received mortal birth. As "the Supreme spoke to me, so do I speak, "and to none do I bear enmity. Whoever "shall call me Paraméswara, he shall sink "into the pit of hell: know, that I am only "the servant of the Supreme, and concerning this entertain no doubt. As God "spoke, I announce unto the world, and "remain not silent in the world of men.

"As God spoke, so do I declare, and I "regard no person's word. I wear my "dress in nobody's fashion, but follow that "appointed by the Supreme. I perform "no worship to stones, nor imitate the "ceremonies of any one. I pronounce "the infinite name, and have attained to "the supreme Being. I wear no bristling "locks on my head, nor adorn myself with "ear-rings. I receive no person's words in "my ears; but as the Lord speaks, I act. "I meditate on the sole name, and attain "my object. To no other do I perform "the Jáp, in no other do I confide: I "meditate on the infinite name, and attain "the supreme light. On no other do I "meditate; the name of no other do I "pronounce.

"For this sole reason, to establish virtue, "was I sent into the world by Gúrú Déva. "'Every where,' said he, 'establish virtue, "and exterminate the wicked and vitious.' "For this purpose have I received mortal "birth; and this let all the virtuous under-"stand. To establish virtue, to exalt piety, "and to extirpate the vitious utterly. "Every former Avatár established his own "Jáp; but no one punished the irreligious, "no one established both the principles "and practice of virtue, (Dherm Carm). "Every holy man (Ghóus), and prophet

" (Ambia), attempted only to establish his " own reputation in the world; but no one " comprehended the supreme Being, or " understood the true principles or practice " of virtue. The doctrine of no other is of " any avail: this doctrine fix in your minds. " There is no benefit in any other doctrine, " this fix in your minds.

" Whoever reads the Korán, whoever " reads the Purán, neither of them shall " escape death, and nothing but virtue " shall avail at last. Millions of men may " read the Kóran, they may read innu- " merable Puráns; but it shall be of no " avail in the life to come, and the power " of destiny shall prevail over them."

Gúrú Góvind, after this account of the origin of his mission, gives a short account of his birth and succession to the spiritual duties at his father's death.

" At the command of God I received " mortal birth, and came into the world.

"This I now declare briefly; attend to "what I speak.

"My father journeyed towards the East, "performing ablution in all the sacred "springs. When he arrived at Triveni, "he spent a day in acts of devotion and "charity. On that occasion was I mani-"fested. In the town of Patna I received "a body. Then the Madra Des received "me, and nurses nursed me tenderly, and "tended me with great care, instructing "me attentively every day. When I "reached the age of Dherm and Carm "(principles and practice), my father de-"parted to the Déva Lóca. When I was "invested with the dignity of Rája, I "established virtue to the utmost of my "power. I addicted myself to every spe-"cies of hunting in the forests, and daily "killed the bear and the stag. When I "had become acquainted with that coun-"try, I proceeded to the city of Pávatá,

" where I amused myself on the banks of
" the Calindri, and viewed every kind of
" spectacle. There I slew a great number
" of tigers; and, in various modes, hunted
" the bear."

The above passages will convey an idea of that impression which Gúrú Góvind gave his followers of his divine mission. I shall shortly enumerate those alterations he made in the usages of the Sikhs, whom it was his object to render, through the means of religious enthusiasm, a warlike race.

Though Gúrú Góvind was brought up in the religion of Nánac, he appears, from having been educated among the Hindú priests of Mathura, to have been deeply tainted with their superstitious belief; and he was, perhaps, induced by considerations of policy, to lean still more strongly to their prejudices, in order to induce them to become converts to that religious military community, by means of which it was his object to destroy the Muhammedan power.

The principal of the religious institutions of Gúrú Góvind, is that of the Páhal,—the ceremony by which a convert is initiated into the tribe of Sikhs; or, more properly speaking, that of Singhs. The meaning of this institution is to make the convert a member of the Khálsa, or Sikh commonwealth, which he can only become by assenting to certain observances; the devoting himself to arms for the defence of the commonwealth, and the destruction of its enemies; the wearing his hair, and putting on a blue dress*.

* It] has been before stated, that all the followers of Góvind do not now wear the blue dress, but they all wear their hair; and their jealous regard of it is not to be described. Three inferior agents of Sikh chiefs were one day in my tent; one of them was a Khálsa Singh, and the two others of the Khalása tribe of Sikhs. I was laughing and joking with the Khálsa Singh, who said

The mode in which Gúrú Góvind first initiated his converts, is described by a Sikh writer; and, as I believe it is nearly the same as that now observed, I shall shortly state it as he has described it. Gúrú Góvind, he says, after his arrival at Mak'-

he had been ordered to attend me to Calcutta. Among other subjects of our mirth, I rallied him on trusting himself so much in my power. "Why, what is the "worst," said he, "that you can do to me, when "I am at such a distance from home?" I passed my hand across my chin, imitating the act of shaving. The man's face was in an instant distorted with rage, and his sword half drawn. "You are ignorant," said he to me, "of the offence you have given. I cannot "strike you, who are above me, and the friend of my "master and the state. But no power," he added, "shall save these fellows," alluding to the two Khalása Sikhs, "from my revenge, for having dared to "smile at your action." It was with the greatest difficulty, and only by the good offices of some Sikh chiefs, that I was able to pacify the wounded honour of this Singh.

haval, initiated five converts, and gave them instructions how to initiate others. The mode is as follows. The convert is told that he must allow his hair to grow. He must clothe himself from head to foot in blue clothes. He is then presented with the five weapons: a sword, a firelock, a bow and arrow, and a pike*. One of those who initiate him then says, "The "Gúrú is thy holy teacher, and thou art "his Sikh or disciple." Some sugar and water is put into a cup, and stirred round with a steel knife, or dagger, and some of the first chapters of the Adí-Grant'h, and the first chapters of the Dasama Pádsháh ka Grant'h, are read; and those who

* The goddess of courage, Bhavani Durgá, represented in the Dasama Pádsháh ka Grant'h, or book of kings of Gúrú Góvind, as the soul of arms, or tutelary goddess of war, and is thus addressed: "Thou art the "edge of the sword, thou art the arrow, the sword, "the knife, and the dagger."

perform the initiation exclaim, *Wa! Gúrúji ka Khálsa! Wa! Gúrúji kí Fateh!* (Success to the state of the Gúrú! Victory attend the Gúrú!) After this exclamation has been repeated five times, they say, "This "sherbet is nectar. It is the water of life; "drink it." The disciple obeys; and some sherbet, prepared in a similar manner, is sprinkled over his head and beard. After these ceremonies, the disciple is asked if he consents to be of the faith of Gúrú Góvind. He answers, "I do consent." He is then told, "If you do, you must abandon all "intercourse, and neither eat, drink, nor sit "in company with men of five sects which "I shall name. The first, the Mína D'hír-"mal; who, though of the race of Nánac, "were tempted by avarice to give poison "to Arjun; and, though they did not suc-"ceed, they ought to be expelled from "society. The second are the Musandiá; "a sect who call themselves Gúrús, or "priests, and endeavour to introduce he-

" terodox doctrines*. The third, Rám " Ráyí, the descendants of Rám Ráy, " whose intrigues were the great cause of " the destruction of the holy ruler, Tégh " Singh. The fourth are the Kud i-már, " or destroyers† of their own daughters. " Fifth, the Bhadaní, who shave the hair " of their head and beards." The disciple, after this warning against intercourse with sectaries, or rather schismatics, is instructed in some general precepts, the observance of which regard the welfare of the community into which he has entered. He is told to be gentle and polite to all with whom he converses, to endeavour to attain wisdom, and to emulate the persuasive eloquence of Baba Nánac. He is particularly enjoined, whenever he approaches any of the Sikh temples, to do it with reverence and respect, and to go to Amritsar, to pay his

* Gúrú Góvind put to death many of this tribe.

† This barbarous custom still prevails among the Rájapúts in many parts of Hindústan.

devotions to the Khálsa, or state; the interests of which he is directed, on all occasions, to consider paramount to his own. He is instructed to labour to increase the prosperity of the town of Amritsar; and told, that at every place of worship which he visits he will be conducted in the right path by the Gúrú (Gúrú Góvind). He is instructed to believe, that it is the duty of all those who belong to the Khálsa, or commonwealth of the Sikhs, neither to lament the sacrifice of property, nor of life, in support of each other; and he is directed to read the Adí-Grant'h and Dasama Pádsháh ka Grant'h, every morning and every evening. Whatever he has received from God, he is told it is his duty to share with others. And after the disciple has heard and understood all these and similar precepts, he is declared to be duly initiated.

Gúrú Góvind Singh, agreeably to this Sikh author, after initiating the first five disciples in the mode above stated, ordered the principal persons among them* to initiate him exactly on similar occasions, which he did. The author from whom the above account is taken, states, that when Góvind was at the point of death, he exclaimed, "Wherever five Sikhs are assembled, there I also shall be present!" and, in consequence of this expression, five Sikhs are the number necessary to make a Singh, or convert. By the religious institutions of Gúrú Góvind, proselytes are admitted from all tribes and casts in the universe. The initiation may take place at any time of life, but the children of the Singhs all go through this rite at a very early age.

The leading tenet of Gúrú Góvind's reli-

* Agreeably to this author, Gúrú Góvind was initiated on Friday, the 8th of the month B'hádra, in the year 1753 of the æra of Vicramáditya; and on that day his great work, the Dasama Pádsháh ka Grant'h, or book of the tenth king, was completed.

gious institutions, which obliges his followers to devote themselves to arms, is stated, in one of the chapters of the Dasama Pádsháh ka Grant'h, or book of the tenth king, written in praise of Dúrga B'havání, the goddess of courage: "Dúrga," Gúrú Góvind says, "appeared to me when I "was asleep, arrayed in all her glory. The "goddess put into my hand the hilt of "a bright scimitar, which she had before "held in her own. 'The country of the "Muhammedans,' said the goddess, 'shall "be conquered by thee, and numbers of "that race shall be slain.' After I had "heard this, I exclaimed, 'This steel shall "be the guard to me and my followers, "because, in its lustre, the splendour of "thy countenance, O goddess! is always "reflected*.'"

* An author, whom I have often quoted, says, Gúrú Góvind gave the following injunctions to his followers: "It is right to slay a Muhammedan wher-

The Dasama Pádsháh ka Grant'h of Gúrú Góvind appears, from the extracts which I have seen of it, to abound in fine passages. Its author has borrowed largely from the Sástras of the Brahméns, and the Korán. He praises Nánac as a holy saint, accepted of God; and grounds his faith, like that of his predecessors, upon the adoration of one God; whose power and attributes he however describes by so many Sanscrit names, and with such constant allusions to the Hindú mythology, that it appears often difficult to separate his purer belief from their gross idolatry. He, however, rejects all worship of images, on an opinion taken from one of the ancient Védas, which declares, "that to worship

"ever you meet him. If you meet a Hindú, beat "him and plunder him, and divide his property "among you. Employ your constant effort to destroy "the countries ruled by Muhammedans. If they "oppose you, defeat and slay them."

"an idol made of wood, earth, or stone, is "as foolish as it is impious; for God alone "is deserving of adoration."

The great points, however, by which Gúrú Góvind has separated his followers for ever from the Hindús, are those which have been before stated;—the destruction of the distinction of casts, the admission of proselytes, and the rendering the pursuit of arms not only admissible, but the religious duty of all his followers. Whereas, among the Hindús, agreeable to the Dherma Sástra, (one of the most revered of their sacred writings,) carrying arms on all occasions, as an occupation, is only lawful to the Cshatriya or military tribe. A Bráhmen is allowed to obtain a livelihood by arms, if he can by no other mode. The Vaisya and Súdra are not allowed to make arms their profession, though they may use them in self-defence.

The sacred book of Gúrú Góvind is not confined to religious subjects, or tales of

Hindú mythology, related in his own way; but abounds in accounts of the battles which he fought, and of the actions which were performed by the most valiant of his followers. Courage is, throughout this work, placed above every other virtue; and Góvind, like Muhammed, makes martyrdom for the faith which he taught, the shortest and most certain road to honour in this world, and eternal happiness in the future. The opinion which the Sikhs entertain of Góvind will be best collected from their most esteemed authors.

"Gúrú Góvind Singh," one* of those writers states, "appeared as the tenth "Avatár. He meditated on the Creator "himself, invisible, eternal, and incom- "prehensible. He established the Khálsa, "his own sect, and, by exhibiting singular "energy, leaving the hair on his head, and "seizing the scimitar, he smote every

* B'hai Gúrú Dás Bhalé.

" wicked person. He bound the garment
" of chastity round his loins, grasped the
" sword of valour, and, passing the true
" word of victory, became victorious in
" the field of combat; and seizing the
" Dévatás, his foes, he inflicted on them
" punishment; and, with great success, dif-
" fused the sublime Gúrú Jáp (a mystical
" form of prayer composed by Gúrú Gó-
" vind) through the world. As he was
" born a warlike Singh, he assumed the
" blue dress; and, by destroying the wicked
" Turks, he exalted the name of Hari
" (God). No Sirdar could stand in battle
" against him, but all of them fled; and,
" whether Hindú Rájás, or Muhammedan
" lords, became like dust in his presence.
" The mountains, hearing of him, were
" struck with terror; the whole world was
" affrighted, and the people fled from their
" habitations. In short, such was his fame,
" that they were all thrown into conster-
" nation, and began to say, ' Besides thee,

"O Sat Gúrú! there is no dispeller of "danger.'—Having seized and displayed "his sword, no person could resist his "might."

The same author, in a subsequent passage, gives a very characteristic account of that spirit of hostility which the religion of Gúrú Góvind breathed against the Muhammedans; and of the manner in which it treated those sacred writings, upon which most of the established usages of Hindús are grounded.

"By the command of the Eternal, the "great Gúrú disseminated the true know-"ledge. Full of strength and courage, he "successfully established the Khálsa (or "state). Thus, at once founding the "sect of Singh, he struck the whole world "with awe: overturning temples and sacred "places, tombs and mosques, he levelled "them all with the plain: rejecting the "Védas, the Puráns, the six Sástras, and "the Korán; he abolished the cry of

“ Namáz (Muhammedan prayer), and slew
“ the Sultans; reducing the Mírs and Pírs
“ (the lords and priests of the Muham-
“ medans) to silence, he overturned all
“ their sects; the Moullahs (professors), and
“ the Kázis (judges), were confounded,
“ and found no benefit from their studies.
“ The Bráhmens, the Pandits, and the
“ Jótìshis (or astrologers), had acquired a
“ relish for worldly things: they worship-
“ ped stones and temples, and forgot the
“ Supreme. Thus these two sects, the
“ Muhammedan and Hindú, remained in-
“ volved in delusion and ignorance, when
“ the third sect of the Khálsa originated in
“ purity. When, at the order of Gúrú
“ Góvind, the Singhs seized and displayed
“ the scimitar, then subduing all their
“ enemies, they meditated on the Eternal;
“ and, as soon as the order of the Most
“ High was manifested in the world, cir-
“ cumcision ceased, and the Turks trem-
“ bled, when they saw the ritual of Mu-

"hammed destroyed: then the Nakára "(large drum) of victory sounded through-"out the world, and fear and dread were "abolished. Thus the third sect was "established, and increased greatly in "might."

These extracts, and what I have before stated, will sufficiently show the character of the religious institutions of Gúrú Góvind; which were admirably calculated to awaken, through the means of fanaticism, a spirit of courage and independence, among men who had been content, for ages, with that degraded condition in society, to which they were taught to believe themselves born. The end which Góvind sought, could not, perhaps, have been attained by the employment of other means. Exhortations respecting their civil rights, and the wrongs which they sustained, would have been wasted on minds enslaved by superstition, and who could only be persuaded to assert themselves men, by an impression that it was the will of Heaven they should do so. His success is a strong elucidation of the general character of the Hindú natives of India. That race, though in general mild and peaceable, take the most savage and ferocious turn, when roused to action by the influence of religious feeling.

I have mentioned, in the narrative part of this Sketch, the attempt of the Bairágí Banda to alter the religious institutions of Gúrú Góvind, and its failure. The tribe of Acálís (immortals), who have now assumed a dictatorial sway in all the religious ceremonies at Amritsar, and the Nirmala and Shahid, who read the sacred writings, may hereafter introduce some changes in those usages which the Sikhs revere: but it is probable that the spirit of equality, which has been hitherto considered as the vital principle of the Khálsa or commonwealth, and which makes all Sikhs so reluctant to own either a temporal or spiritual leader, will tend greatly to preserve their institutions from invasion: and it is stated, in a tradition which is universally believed by the Sikhs, and has, indeed, been inserted in their sacred writings, that Gúrú Góvind, when he was asked by his followers, who surrounded his death-bed, to whom he would leave his authority? replied, "I have delivered over the Khálsa (com-"monwealth) to God, who never dies. I "have been your guide, and will still pre-"serve you; read the Grant'h, and attend "to its tenets; and whoever remains true "to the state, him will I aid." From these dying words of Gúrú Góvind, the Sikhs believe themselves to have been placed, by their last and most revered prophet, under the peculiar care of God: and their attachment to this mysterious principle, leads them to consider the Khálsa (or commonwealth) as a theocracy; and such an impression is likely to oppose a very serious obstacle, if not an insuperable barrier, to the designs of any of their chiefs, who may hereafter endeavour to establish an absolute power over the whole nation.

THE END.

BOOKS LATELY PUBLISHED

BY JOHN MURRAY,

50, ALBEMARLE STREET, LONDON.

1. THE QUARTERLY REVIEW; from its Commencement, in 1809, to December 1812. Sixteen Numbers, forming Eight Volumes, 8vo. handsomely printed; price 5l. in extra boards.

New Editions of each Number have been again printed, and they may now be had separately; price 6s.

No. 17 will be published early in February 1813, *and the future Numbers regularly every three months.*

2. SKETCH OF THE POLITICAL HISTORY OF India: From the Introduction of Mr. PITT's Bill, A. D. 1784, to the present Date. By JOHN MALCOLM, Lieutenant-Colonel in the East India Company's Madras Army, Resident at Mysore, and late Envoy to the Court of Persia. Second Edition, royal 8vo. 18s.

3. GEOGRAPHICAL MEMOIR OF THE PERSIAN Empire: interspersed with Accounts of Manners and Customs. By JOHN MACDONALD KINNEIR, Esq. Political Assistant to Brigadier-General MALCOLM, late Envoy to the Court of Persia. Handsomely printed in 4to. with a Map. 3l. 3s.

4. A VOYAGE ROUND THE WORLD, IN THE Years 1803, 4, 5, and 6; by the command of his Imperial Majesty, Alexander I. in the Ships Nadeshda and Neva; under the orders of Captain A. J. VON KRUSENSTERN. Translated from the German, (now printing at Berlin,) by RICHARD BELGRAVE HOPPNER, Esq. Handsomely printed in One large Volume 4to. with Charts, Plates, &c. &c. *In the Press.*

This Voyage is extremely interesting, not only as being the first ever undertaken by Russia round the World, but as replete with accurate and valuable information. Its principal object was to carry out M. De Resanoff, Ambassador Extraordinary from the Court of Russia to the Empire of Japan, with the view of establishing a communication. It contains a particular Account of this Embassy, and an interesting Description of the Manners and Customs of the several Tribes and Nations of the Great Pacific, hitherto so little known.

5. AN ACCOUNT OF THE KINGDOM OF NEPAUL: Being the Substance of Observations made during a Mission to that Country in the Year 1793. By Colonel WILLIAM KIRKPATRICK. In royal 4to. embellished with a large Map and Fifteen Engravings. 2l. 12s. 6d.

6. TWENTY-FOUR LARGE VIEWS IN ARABIA, Abyssinia, and Egypt, &c. Executed from Drawings by HENRY SALT, Esq. who accompanied Lord Valentia on his Travels, and has since been employed on a Mission to Abyssinia.

The Engravings are in the same size and manner as Mr. DANIELL's Oriental Scenery, being 24 by 18 inches. The whole are mounted, and delivered in a portfolio, at the price of Twenty-six Guineas the Set.

7. THE COSTUMES:—Illustrative of the Manners, Habits, and Decorations of the Russians, Turks, Austrians, Chinese, &c. represented in a Series of Three Hundred and Seventy-three Engravings, accurately finished in the Colours of the original Subjects, with short descriptive Essays; forming Seven Volumes, Imperial 4to. as follow:

The COSTUME of CHINA; by Lieutenant-Colonel MASON; from original Drawings, by PEU QUA, of Canton—Six Guineas.

The PUNISHMENTS of CHINA; by the Same—Three Guineas and a Half.

The COSTUME of TURKEY; by OCTAVIAN D'ALVEMART—Eight Guineas.

The COSTUME of RUSSIA—Eight Guineas.

The COSTUME of AUSTRIA—Six Guineas.

The COSTUME of CHINA; by WILLIAM ALEXANDER, Draftsman to the Embassy of Earl Macartney—Six Guineas.

The COSTUME of GREAT BRITAIN; by W. H. PYNE—Nine Pounds.

The price of the complete Set, in extra boards, is Forty-eight Pounds Sixteen Shillings and Sixpence.

Either Volume may be had separately.

---

8. THE COSTUME OF THE ANCIENTS: Consisting of a Series of Three Hundred Engravings in Outline, with some introductory Letter-press. By THOMAS HOPE, Esq. In Two Volumes, royal 4to. 6l. 6s.

The same Work, in Two Volumes, royal 8vo. 2l. 12s. 6d.

---

9. THE HISTORIC GALLERY OF PORTRAITS AND Paintings; or, Graphic Imitations of the finest Specimens of the Arts, ancient and modern; with Descriptions and Remarks, Biographical, Critical, and Explanatory. In Seven Volumes 8vo. Containing more than 500 outline Engravings, executed with peculiar taste and spirit. Price 1l. 4s. each Volume. A few Copies, printed in 4to. may be had, price 2l. 5s. each Volume.

The design of the present publication is to display, in a small compass, the labours of the Historian, combined with the happiest efforts of the pencil. It is intended to contribute to the advancement of science, by presenting to the contemplation of the artist and the connoisseur, specimens of the most esteemed works of the best masters, ancient and modern, both in painting and in sculpture; and by diffusing in a novel and interesting form a knowledge of what for ages has been appreciated and enthusiastically admired, instil into the mind of the mere indifferent observer a taste for the polite arts.

---

10. TRAVELS IN THE ISLAND OF ICELAND during the Summer of the Year 1810. By Sir GEORGE STEUART MACKENZIE, Bart. Fellow of the Royal Society of Edinburgh, &c. &c. In One Volume, 4to. embellished with Two Maps, Fifteen Plates, (many finely coloured), and Fifteen Vignettes. Second Edition. 3l. 3s.

---

11. THE BATTLES OF TALAVERA: a Poem, with Notes. The Ninth London Edition; with important Additions and Corrections. To which are now added TRAFALGAR, and other Poems. With a Portrait of Lord WELLINGTON, from an original Bust. Handsomely printed in 4to. 15s.

12. **ROMANCES: Consisting of MEJNOUN and LEILA, a Persian Romance, interspersed with Notes and Poetry descriptive of Oriental Scenery.—LOVE and HUMILITY; a Roman Romance.—The LOVERS; or, The BIRTH of the PLEASING ARTS; an Arcadian Romance. By I. D'ISRAELI, Esq. Third Edition. With an Engraving, after a design by Westall. Foolscap 8vo. 7s. 6d.**

---

13. **CHILDE HAROLD'S PILGRIMAGE. A Romaunt. Written during the Author's Travels in Portugal, Spain, Albania, and some of the most interesting Parts of Greece. With Notes. To which are added, a few Miscellaneous Poems, and Translations of modern Greek Songs, written chiefly abroad: and an Appendix, containing Observations on modern Greek Literature, with a short Catalogue of Romaic Authors. By the Right Hon. Lord BYRON. Fifth Edition. Handsomely printed in 8vo. 12s.**

---

14. **THE LIFE OF NELSON. Beautifully printed in One Volume, small 8vo. with Plates, 7s. 6d.**

Many Lives of NELSON have been written: one is yet wanting, clear and concise enough to become a Manual for the young Sailor, which he may carry about with him till he has treasured up the example in his memory and in his heart. In attempting such a Work, the Author proposes to himself to write the Eulogy of our great Naval Hero; for the best Eulogy of NELSON is the faithful history of his actions; the best history is that which shall relate them most perspicuously.

A very few Copies are printed on large paper, price 12s.

---

15. **LIFE OF MICHEL ANGELO BUONARROTI; comprising his Letters, Poetry, &c. Specimens of which are translated by SOUTHEY and WORDSWORTH into English Verse; containing also a critical Disquisition on his Merit as a Sculptor, a Painter, an Architect, and a Poet. By R. DUPPA, Esq. The Second Edition, elegantly printed in Imperial 4to. by Bensley; containing a Portrait of Michel Angelo, by BARTOLOZZI, and Fifty other Engravings. 3l. 13s. 6d.**

---

16. **COLLECTIONS FROM THE DEIPHNOSOPHISTS, or Banquet of the Gods, of ATHENÆUS. Translated from the original Greek, by THOMAS EAGLES, Esq. F.R.S. beautifully printed in Two Volumes, post 8vo. 18s.**

This Work is peculiarly interesting, from its lively exhibition of various convivial customs, which prevailed in different countries in different periods: interspersed with passages of exquisite Poetry.

---

17. **CALAMITIES OF AUTHORS: Including some Inquiries respecting their MORAL and LITERARY Characters. By the Author of CURIOSITIES of LITERATURE. Neatly printed in Two Volumes, small 8vo. 16s.**

---

18. **TALES OF THE EAST: Containing upwards of One Thousand Stories: comprising the whole of the Arabian, Persian, Turkish, Mogul, Tartarian, and Chinese Tales: besides a number of original Translations and Reprints of interesting but little known Eastern Romances. Elegantly printed by Ballantyne, in Three Volumes super-royal 8vo. double columns. 3l. 18s.**

This Work will be continued till a Series of our best Novels and Romances be completed, and may extend probably to Fifteen Volumes, each portion of which will be distinct and complete in itself, and sold separately.